A HAR

JOY

Karla –
Happy 39th
Sept 2006
Next yr. begins one!
Youre a delight!
God made "u"
Very Special!!!!
"♡-2-u"
Maxine

A HARVEST OF JOY

Tools to Cultivate the Fruit of the Spirit

REBEKAH MONTGOMERY

ISBN 1-57748-845-8

Unless otherwise noted, all Scripture quotations are taken from the King James Version of the Bible, except those marked NIV, which are from the New International Version.

Published by Promise Press, an imprint of Barbour Publishing, Inc., P.O. Box 719, Uhrichsville, Ohio 44683 http://www.barbourbooks.com

Printed in the United States of America.

Dedication

To my sisters in the flesh and in the Spirit—
Rose, Ruth, Mary, Donna, Sherry, Barb, Char,
Lou, Laurie, Lisa, Charlotte, Angie, Christine, Amy B.,
Cathy L., Katie W., Katie B., Deb S., Cathy P., Pam,
Edie, Arlene, Janelle, Amy C., Glenna, Mary N., Althea,
Chrissie, Bridget, Sharon, Becky D., Becky K., Nancy S.,
and my one and only Mom, Catherine Willson Binkley.

Chapter 1

What Kind of Fruit is Joy?

Joy to the world! the Lord is come!
Let earth receive her King;
Let every heart prepare Him room,
And heav'n and nature sing.

Joy to the earth! the Savior reigns!
Let men their songs employ,
While fields and floods, rocks, hills, and plains,
Repeat the sounding joy.

No more let sins and sorrows grow,
Nor thorns infest the ground;
He comes to make His blessings flow
Far as the curse is found.

He rules the world with truth and grace,
And makes the nations prove
The glories of His righteousness,
And wonders of His love.
ISAAC WATTS

The Difference Between Joy and Happiness

Every year on our two-and-a-half-acre bit of country paradise, my husband planted a garden big enough to feed a small Third World nation. Once the seeds were in the ground, he turned the care and feeding of the plants over to me from germination to harvest. He would occasionally run the tiller down the rows, but between the plants, the hoeing was all mine. So in the early morning hours while our babies were still asleep, before the summer sun heated to its full fury, I would slip on my old shoes, grab the hoe, and go out to the vegetable garden for a *tete-à-tete* with the weeds.

As I chopped out the Canadian thistles and tangled wild morning glory vines, I couldn't help but marvel over the divine bit of enchantment that transformed an insignificant kernel of corn into little green ribbons of leaves and then into fully mature stalks complete with tassels, silk, ears, and edible kernels. Tomatoes, green beans, and peppers were also marvels, but zucchini truly amazed me. Almost before my very eyes, I could see it bloom, produce fruit, and mature into over-grown seedpods!

Most vegetables did well in our waxy clay soil, but certain ones—like melons, or root crops such as carrots, and eggplant—required special tending to come to fruition. The wild rabbits loved tender eggplant seedlings, and unless I chained a hungry Doberman to the plants, the bunnies ate them down to the quick. Melons and root crops require sandy, loose soil, and although we could get them to grow, we didn't reap a particularly satisfactory crop unless I especially prepared planting spots for them by spading in fertilizer, sand, and peat. Then they did fine.

Joy, one of the fruits of the Spirit, is a little like my garden. Its growth in our lives is miraculous and amazing—but it won't grow automatically; it needs particular growing conditions if it is to bloom and bear fruit.

Other aspects of my garden remind me of joy as well. While some people are just naturally happy and easily derive satisfaction from the little things in life, God-grown joy is as different from happiness as gourds are from squash. Happiness may bear a cursory resemblance to joy, but that's as far as it goes.

Gourds are not nourishing, and in some cases, they're even

poisonous. You can make a few useful items out of them, but they are mostly decorative. Happiness is like that. It looks good; it has its sphere of usefulness; but its value is limited.

Squash, on the other hand, keeps well and is a terrific source of vitamins. You can eat it raw, baked in the shell, or make all manner of healthy foods out of it from desserts to main courses. That is very much the case with joy, for it endures and nourishes us. As I said, at first glance, it may look a lot like happiness, but unlike happiness, joy has wonderful sustaining power for the human soul.

So how do we cultivate true joy in our lives? Well, actually, it's not something we can produce by ourselves, no matter how hard we try. Instead, anywhere the Spirit of God dwells, joy will automatically be the result. The Holy Spirit chops out the weeds and breaks up the hardened clay in our hearts, sifting in better qualities. . .so that joy and the other spiritual fruit will find hospitable growing conditions. Often times—very often — He uses troubles and trials like hoes to hew out the weeds of bad habits, to break up the hardened soil of selfishness to make a spot for joy to flourish.

Sometimes it takes a long time for joy to appear in a certain area of life. Other times, it springs up overnight and bears fruit all at once (like my zucchini plants). But wherever the Spirit of God is, joy will result and it is a useful, delicious, and eternal fruit—well worth our pain and well worth the labor of the Master Gardener.

There is a joy
which is not given to the ungodly,
but to those who love Thee
for Thine own sake,
whose joy Thou Thyself art.
And this is the happy life,
to rejoice to Thee, of Thee, for Thee;
this it is, and there is no other.

AUGUSTINE

When we try to reach happiness on cheap terms, what we get is bound to be cheap. DAVID ROBERTS

Joy is not found by making the acquisition of it our focus. It is found by making God our focus and finding Him. Joy will automatically result because wherever God is, there is joy!

When I think of God, my heart is so full of joy that the notes leap and dance as they leave my pen; and since God has given me a cheerful heart, I serve Him with a cheerful spirit.

FRANZ JOSEPH HAYDN

Joy is
the flag that's flying
when the King is home.

MARY CROWLEY

So I say, live by the Spirit, and you will not gratify the desires of the sinful nature. For the sinful nature desires what is contrary to the Spirit. . . . They are in conflict with each other, so that you do not do what you want.

The acts of the sinful nature are obvious: sexual immorality, impurity and debauchery; idolatry and witchcraft; hatred, discord, jealousy, fits of rage, selfish ambition, dissensions, factions and envy; drunkenness, orgies, and the like. I warn you, as I did before, that those who live like this will not inherit the kingdom of God.

But the fruit of the Spirit is. . .joy.

GALATIANS 5:16–17, 19–22 NIV

Created for Joy

At daybreak on Friday morning of creation, the Lord God Almighty reached out of heaven and took a scoop of clay—red clay, a plentiful variety that contains fine bits of grit for strength but is sometimes astonishingly stubborn to mold. Every other element of the new creation had been spoken into existence; at the mere Word of God, all sprang to life. But there was one job that God reserved for His own two hands.

As He brought the handful of clay up to heaven, the bright beings gathered around to watch. Over the last five days, they had observed the universe and earth burst into existence at the sound of His voice, and they had been delighted and amazed, but now on this sixth day He was doing something very new and they wanted to observe closely.

With rapt concentration, He began to shape the clay, pinching up areas, smoothing down others. The bright ones had never seen Him put so much attention and effort into any one creation as He did this, and they wondered what He was making, what was so important about this creation that He would form it personally instead of letting it spring from His Words. They longed to ask, "Lord God, why do you spend so much time and care on a lump of clay?" but because in eternity past they had had the pleasure and surprise of watching His purposes unfold in His own season, they chose not to rob themselves of future wonder.

The eternal day wore on as the Almighty continued His labor. Under His fingertips, the creation took clearer shape and form, and the bright ones were increasingly awed. In many respects, the lump now had some of the appearance of a bright one, but there were paradoxical differences. It was stronger than an angel, but also weaker; it was smaller than the bright ones, but also larger. And it bore the image of God. None of the bright ones bore the image of God, and to see His likeness in cold, dead clay was a disconcerting shock to them.

The sun was setting on the planet below as the Lord God put the finishing touches on the piece of clay. He had painstakingly examined the tiniest crevices, and He was pleased with the result. As He held it in His hand, observing it from every angle, a tender smile played across His face. *Why,* wondered the bright ones, *does He love this lump of clay so much?* But this had been a day unlike any other in all of eternity, and while they knew His ways were beyond theirs, what happened next made them clap their hands and shout with joy.

Cupping His hands gently, the Lord God Almighty held the lump close to His own face and gently breathed the breath of life into the clay nostrils. Life and color began from the nostrils and gradually spread down until the entire lump of cold clay became a living man.

Then the Lord God did something else odd. He gently

placed the living man into His Son's hands. The Son held the man before His face and waited. The man awakened slowly, stretching, yawning, making soft grunting noises as the Lord God smilingly watched on from a distance.

Finally, the man opened his eyes and looked full into the face of the Son. As the first sight of his newly formed eyes, the Son's face was forever imprinted upon the man's soul. No matter how far from His presence he strayed, no matter whether he made his bed in the deepest hell, he would forever search for the Son's face and never have joy unless he could see Him.

But now, fresh from the Creator's fingertips, the man was relaxed, at peace, but full of curious wonder, as he lay in the hands of the Son and regarded his Maker.

At long last, the Lord God, the Son, and the Holy Spirit spoke, their voices rumbling in harmony through the heavens and echoing off the stars: "Adam," They said, and all the bright ones instantly recognized that God was naming the man for the red clay from which he had been formed. "Welcome to the world We have made for you! Come experience the joy for which We have created you."

In that moment when all creation was pristine and unsullied, as the ancestor of all mortal souls rested in the hands of God, the mind of Jehovah knew you and me. He counted the hours of our lives. He knew that sin would eventually squeeze the spirit from our flesh and we would return to dust and lifeless clay.

But from the foundations of the world, before the first sin, the Son was slain to atone for them. Our frailty will not permit us to see God's face now, but through Jesus we would know Him because the Word would become flesh and make His dwelling among us. We would behold His glory, the glory of the One and Only who came from the Father, full of grace and truth.

The Son had a goal in coming to earth that was given Him by the Father:

To show us His Face once more so we could again know joy!

Based on GENESIS 1, JOB 38, and JOHN 1

Don't pursue joy: Pursue Christ. If you seek the gift alone, it will flee from you. If you seek Christ alone, the gift will come to you. Seek the Giver, not the gift. You were created for joy. Look for Him.

Is it actually possible that God's people should be living always in the joy and strength of their God? Every believing heart must answer, It is possible.

ANDREW MURRAY

Typical joy—the usual garden variety—is found scattered like dandelions all over the human experience in a variety of forms: momentary splashes of joy caused by a child's good school report card, by hot coffee and an intimate chat with a good friend, by a cozy cuddle on a cold night, or by a child learning to tie his shoes. These small, ordinary joys are as important as the bigger ones, and we need to remember that they, too, are blessings sprinkled in our lives by a loving God.

Then there are the profound life-altering joys—a wedding, the birth of a healthy baby, a new job, the achievement of a goal long pursued. These, too, are gifts from God, and our delight pleases Him.

But all these joys are still tied to earthly blessings. Spiritual joy, grown completely by the Holy Spirit alive in our hearts, has a far different flavor. It is a unique variety, developed patiently for us over the course of human history in three separate gardens.

This joy germinated in the Garden of Eden. It bloomed in the Garden of Gethsemene. And it came to sweet fruition in the garden tomb where Jesus rose from the dead. Each step of its development was overseen by the Master Gardener Who planted it, watered it with His own sweat and tears, then picked it and offered it to us with His own nail-scarred but resurrected hands. Because of Christ, this joy will be ours for eternity.

What are the defining features of divine joy? Well, we can recognize its presence in our lives by the healing it brings from the Great Physician. What is more, it restores our souls. It brings us eternal hope from the risen Christ. It provides us with sustenance from the All-Sufficient One. It gives direction from the Shepherd. It is rooted in our deepest identities in the Lord, and it is the banner that waves over our lives. It is protection against life's dangers, for it springs from our Shield and Defender. It is support from the Chief Cornerstone. It is shade in a weary land. It comes to us even in the Father's correction. It brings us serenity from the Prince of Peace. And we find it whenever we bow to the King of Kings, when we submit to the Lord of Lords. It is Jesus in our lives.

Thou wilt shew me
the path of life:
in thy presence is fulness of joy;
at thy right hand there are
pleasures for evermore.

PSALM 16:11

"In thy presence is fullness of joy," and fullness of joy is nowhere else. Just as the simple presence of the mother makes the child's joy, so does the simple fact of God's presence with us make our joy. The mother may not make a single promise to the child, nor explain any of her plans or purposes, but she is, and that is enough for the child. The child rejoices in the mother; not in her promises, but in herself. And to the child, there is behind all that changes and can change, the one unchangeable joy of mother's existence. While the mother lives, the child will be cared for; and the child knows this, instinctively, if not intelligently, and rejoices in knowing it. And to the children of God as well, there is behind all that changes and can change, the one unchangeable joy that God is. And while He is, His children will be cared for, and they ought to know it and rejoice in it, instinctively and far more intelligently than the child of human parents. For what else can God do, being what He is? Neglect, indifference, forgetfulness, ignorance, are all impossible to Him. He knows everything, He cares about everything. He can manage everything, and He loves us! Surely this is enough for a "fullness of joy" beyond the power of words to express. HANNAH WHITALL SMITH

Happiness? Or Joy?

Joy is not happiness. Happiness springs from circumstances whereas the Spirit of God implants joy. Happiness betrays its character with its root word—*hap*—which is just another word for luck. Other words with the same root are happenstance, hapless, haphazard, haply. The implication with these words is that happiness merely occurs, with no rhyme or reason.

But joy is God's design for you. He didn't blueprint you to be occasionally happy while you are blown about by the winds of chance and swept by the accidental currents of circumstance. He planned you for joy—true joy unchanged by the tides.

One of the hallmarks of Christian believers is that they are joyful people. Some people characterize Christians as dour, sour, pallid, and lifeless. But they are mistaking the religious for the Christian.

The life-giving, joyful, loving Spirit of God fills a Christian. If you do not have this joy within you, with what are you filled?

Wait for the Spirit's joy. Don't settle for mere happiness.

Happiness is usually caused by circumstances. When things are going great, we feel happy; when life is unpleasant, we are depressed. Supernatural joy, however, enables us to experience a deeper joy that is not so dependent on our

circumstances. As we live by correct priorities, cultivating our relationship with Christ on a daily basis, we will begin to experience a quiet joy resulting from a sense of security that we belong to God, and He is indeed in control of our lives. When we focus on this security, we will be free to relax and trust Him in whatever situation we find ourselves. We will not always feel happy, but we will have a deeper sense of joy that we belong to Christ and that His plans for us are good. God's joy is supernatural. His joy is also refreshing.
SUSAN ALEXANDER YATES

Simply Dispensed Joy—The Principle of the Smiley Face

It was early, insanely early, about five A.M. on a winter morning so cold that I could see little smoky wisps of my breath in the upstairs bedroom. I hurriedly pulled on my winter robe and stepped downstairs to throw some more wood in the stove to take off the chill before the rest of the family got up. Through Jack Frost's handiwork on the kitchen window, I vainly tried to read the outside thermometer. I could make out the thirty-two-degree marker, and I located zero, but the mercury itself was nowhere to be seen. I could only conclude it had slid to the very bottom of the thermometer and frozen in the bulb. The weather had been like that for days, and because I hate to be cold, I was feeling grouchy about facing another shivery day. I thought hibernation sounded like a wonderful idea.

I backed up to the wood stove. The heat felt so good that I briefly considered getting a good book and spending the day reading, sitting cross-legged on the griddle. I felt it would only begin to thaw me out.

Strange how responsibilities can nag at a person—even from a considerable distance and especially when you prefer to be deaf to them.

At the moment, my little group of animals in the barn were calling to me in my mind. The chickens, rabbits, and milk goat that appeared to be such lovely, helpful creatures in the summer now seemed like terrible nuisances in winter when I had to wade through subzero gale force winds and snow to bring water and feed to them.

Coffee. A cup of coffee first, I thought. I needed coffee before I faced my arctic adventure.

As I reached to open the cupboard, I was stopped short. There, stuck on the doorknob, was a tiny smiley face. It was drawn on craft paper with a pen, rough-cut, and secured to the knob with masking tape. I laughed out loud at the sight of it. I instantly recognized the drawing technique as well as the mental gymnastics that thought up this droll bit of decor as belonging to my budding artist and ten-year-old daughter Mary. She was—and is—a whimsical, zany sort, and this was just the sort of thing she'd do.

Very funny, Mary! thought I. *Congratulations on a good practical joke!*

My mood considerably lightened, I yanked open the cupboard door. A large smiley face greeted me from the backside of the cupboard door. I laughed again. Then I reached for my favorite coffee mug. Stuck to the bottom of the inside was yet another roguishly happy countenance. What on earth? On a hunch, I grabbed another cup. It, too, wore a smiley face as did every cup and glass on the shelf. I was impressed. Although they were quickly, easily made, the sheer number of happy faces it took to cheer up the cupboard was impressive!

I thought I had come to the end of them until I opened the refrigerator for a splash of milk. The carton was smiling. I pulled out a stool to sit at the counter. A smiley face seat cover greeted me. Slowly, I discovered that she'd put them everywhere—on cereal boxes, apples, the bread bag, drawn on sticks of butter, on houseplants, stuck in the middle of the telephone dial. When had she done all of this?

Pondering this, I went to get my stock water bucket. A smiley face greeted me from the bottom. I pulled on my chore coverall. A smiley face was tucked inside each pocket. I pulled out my gloves. A smiley face adorned each fingertip. As I opened the backdoor and braced myself for an icy blast, I couldn't help but wonder if my animals would be sporting smiles.

They weren't—but a whole lot of other things were! When we moved from that house some ten years later, I was still finding smiley faces, and every time I uncovered them, they cheered me all over again!

Later that morning when I got Mary up for school, I discovered the origin of the smiley faces. She'd had insomnia the night before. She didn't want to wake me—bless her! I had a two-year-old at the time—so she decided to spread a little cheer. Thus: smiley faces everywhere her agile little mind thought to put them. "They made me happy, and pretty soon, I could sleep," she told me, her impish eyes sparkling.

What could have been a wasted, sleepless night turned into a blessing, not only because it cheered me up in the morning, but because it spawned the "principle of the smiley face," which is: When you are sad, give happiness. When you are lonely, befriend. When you are troubled, give comfort. When you need help, offer some. When you are joyless, give joy.

Jesus knew the "principle of the smiley face," but He stated it differently: "Give, and it will be given to you. A good measure, pressed down, shaken together, and running over, will be poured into your lap. For with the measure you use, it will be measured to you" (Luke 6:38 NIV).

Joy fits so snugly into His definition that it can be inserted into the verse: Give joy, and it shall be given unto you.

A good measure of joy, pressed down, and shaken together, and running over, will be poured into your lap. For with the same measure that you give joy, it will be measured to you again.

Each time, the "principle of the smiley face" holds up. When I find myself with a case of cabin fever, I reach for the phone and call someone I know who is truly locked in the house for the winter. When I find myself sad, I send a word of comfort via a greeting card to someone who is mourning. Or I visit them, make a phone call, or send a bouquet. When I need joy, I try to give it to someone else. Then surprise! It springs up in my own heart!

> *The ordinary group of worshipping Christians, as the preacher sees them from the pulpit, does not look like a collection of very joyful people; in fact, they look on the whole rather sad, tired, depressed people. It is certain that such people will never win the world for Christ. . . . It is no use trying to pretend: we may speak of joy and preach about it: but, unless we really have the joy of Christ in our hearts and manifest it, our words will carry no conviction to our hearers.*
>
> STEPHEN NEILL
> *The Christian Character*

The Mystery of Joy and Blessing

Early in Jesus' ministry, He gave a formal statement of His teachings about God. This statement is usually called the Sermon on the Mount. At the beginning of His sermon, as recorded in Matthew, are a series of nine remarkable statements that spell out the blessings—or the joys—available to a Christian believer. In nearly every case, they fly in the face of human reasoning, dramatically proving once again God's thoughts are not our thoughts and our ways are not His.

In many translations, the first part of each statement begins with "Blessed are. . ." and concludes with the reward that follows. If we take the first phrase apart, we see that "blessed" in each case means "God-given bliss" or "supernatural joy." Each statement could well have begun with "Oh, the God-given bliss of those who. . ." or "Oh, the supernatural joy of those who. . . ."

As we look closely at each of these statements by the Master, we also see that each statement deals with the normal conflicts and sorrows of this life and how God turns them into joy!

Christ is a God of joy. . . . A Christian should be and
must be a person of joy.
The devil is the spirit of sadness, but God is the Spirit of
joy, and he is our salvation.
We have more occasion for joy than sadness. The reason is

we believe in the living God, and Christ lives, and we shall live also.

MARTIN LUTHER

God-Given Bliss, Supernatural Joy

Oh, the supernatural joy of those who realize their need for God, for theirs is the kingdom of heaven!
Oh, the God-given bliss of those who mourn, for God will comfort them!
Oh, the supernatural joy of those who are joyful and humble, for the whole earth will belong to them!
Oh, the God-given bliss of those who are hungry and thirsty for justice, for they will be filled!
Oh, the supernatural joy of those who show mercy to others, for mercy will be given to them!
Oh, the God-given bliss of those whose hearts are pure, for they will see God!
Oh, the supernatural joy of those who work for peace, for they will be called the children of God!
Oh, the God-given bliss of those who run into hard times because they are living for God, for the kingdom of heaven is theirs!

MATTHEW 5:3–10 (PARAPHRASED)

Joyfully Blessed

"You must believe in yourself!" a mother exhorted her child. "You must believe that you are a good person and capable of doing great things!"

Good advice? Popular counsel, perhaps, but not true. Can the child—by her own efforts—make herself pleasing to God? Can she blaze a new path to heaven using her own navigational tools?

The joyfully blessed know the truth: In us dwells no good thing. Our righteousness is as filthy rags. Only by grace are we admitted to heaven, not through our own works, or we would boast. We know we can't earn heaven, find it on our own, seize it by force, buy it, steal it, or charm or bribe our way into it.

The poor in spirit inherit the kingdom of heaven as a gift of God because regardless of what we know about our own self-worth, we are beloved of God. That's what grace is all about. And therein is joy!

Joy does not depend on the hours that you spend watching sports or movies. It doesn't depend on the time you spend at work. It has nothing to do with the novels you read, or with conversations with friends and acquaintances. It doesn't spring from the time you spend pursuing hobbies. All these things may bring you pleasure—but you'll never reap eternal joy from them. You'll only find eternal joy in the Person of Jesus Christ.

Discover Him between the covers of the Bible.

The joy Christ gives is not dependent upon anything the world gives—or withholds.

A Sterile Vine

The Man with Everything but Joy

"Your son!" the other mothers said to his mother. "Such a good boy! Does he have a girlfriend?"

And from all outside appearances, he did look like a good catch. Nearly any mother would have considered him ideal husband material for her daughter. He was wealthy, powerful, kind to his parents, morally clean, honest, religious—a genuine first century Eagle Scout. He'd made a lifetime career out of doing the right thing.

Hard to believe, but the man himself felt empty. There was something missing in his life. He just couldn't put his finger on it.

He'd chased this elusive, unnamed butterfly from his childhood, except that in the naïve days of his youth, he had deceived himself into believing that there was actually a possibility of finding it. His parents had said, "Be a good boy." So he was good. His teachers instructed him to study hard. So he had. The priests said, "Follow the Law." So he'd tried. When money and authority tantalized him, promised the illusionary missing piece, he'd chased them. Once they were in his grasp, they dissolved into ashes.

What was wrong?

He'd heard quite a lot about the Teacher from Nazareth, and frankly, Jesus had him baffled. Here was the Man who could have it all. He had the charisma to persuade people to leave their livelihood, home, and hearth to lead a nomad's life following Him around the country. He certainly had the intelligence and political savvy to lead a nation—nay, the world! He could make speeches that moved the multitudes. He taught with far greater authority than the most learned priest. He could make wine out of water or walk on it—whichever the occasion demanded, feed five thousand people with a couple of fish sandwiches, make the blind see, and bring the dead back to life. He could inspire people to change their lives. He could do all of that and more—effortlessly—but He seemed to be pulling toward something else. He seemed to know the name of the butterfly, could call it to Him, and use its wings to soar. He seemed to know what happiness, true happiness, was all about.

So the man carefully observed Jesus for a time. And he was impressed.

However, when he spotted Jesus rather pointedly ignoring

some prominent Pharisees but giving His full attention to a crowd of grimy little children, he almost dismissed Him as a genuine crackpot. Talking to children! Holding them on His lap! What a waste of time! The man stood there, stunned by the sight. Then Jesus and the crowd moved on.

He'd come this far to ask the question; regardless of the opportunities Jesus seemed to be throwing away, he should, at very least, seize the moment. He ran to catch up, then fell on his knees before Jesus.

"Good teacher," he asked, "what should I do to inherit eternal life?"

Jesus curiously regarded the young man. "Why do you call me good?" Jesus asked him. "No one is good—except God alone."

The man paused. He understood exactly the implications of the question Jesus was posing to him: "Am I God? Do you think I have the authority to tell you what to do with your life? Am I the Author of life? If so, do I know what you should do with your life? And if I am God, will you obey Me?" The man didn't answer: He just stared at Jesus' feet.

"All right, then," said Jesus, seeing that the young man was debating how to answer. "You know the commandments: Do not murder, do not commit adultery, do not steal, do not give false testimony, do not defraud, honor your father and mother."

Now, at last, the young man felt he was on solid footing.

"Teacher," he declared earnestly, "all these I have kept since I was a boy!"

Thoughtfully, Jesus regarded the man. Here before Him was a nice person, an earnest soul, a thoroughly loveable man. Jesus didn't want to see him unhappy; He knew precisely what stood between the man and joy.

"There is one thing you lack," He said. The man started. How did Jesus know about that one thing he had been pursuing all his life? Perhaps He was God! He now gave Jesus his full attention.

Then He spoke: "Go, sell everything you have and give to the poor and you will have treasure in heaven. Then come, follow Me."

The man's face fell at Jesus' words. *No!* he thought, *I can't do that! I don't want my life to be emptier; I want it to be fuller! How can it be fuller if I give up my things? It takes money, power, and something more—that intangible something more—to be happy. Joy comes from without; not from within! Jesus is a poor man with no power or possessions. He simply doesn't understand!*

However, better than anyone, Jesus knew the cost of His request. After all, Jesus Himself had left His position in glory. He had turned His back on all the riches of heaven. He had surrendered His life.

Yet, He also understood and was experiencing the two-pronged joy of obedience to God and service to mankind, and He knew this man would finally experience true, rapturous joy if He followed His example.

Yet, without another word, the man turned away.

Sorrow etched the face of Jesus as he watched him leave. The man would have made a wonderful follower! And in following Him, he would have found the joy for which he was seeking.

How many times have we missed lasting satisfaction because we could not, would not say "Yes!" to Jesus? How many times have we deprived our souls of delight because we would not turn loose of some earthly, corrupting thing?

To us, as to the rich young man, Jesus extends the paradoxical key to the Kingdom and joy: "If any man will come after Me, let him deny himself, and take up his cross, and follow Me. For whosoever will save his life shall lose it: and whosoever will lose his life for my sake shall find it. For what is a man profited, if he shall gain the whole world, and lose his own soul? or what shall a man give in exchange for his soul?"

Based on MARK 10, MATTHEW 16:24–26

The only thing that can bring unfailing joy to the soul is to understand and know God. . . . When all else is gone, God is still left. Nothing changes Him. He is the same yesterday, today, and forever, and in Him is no variableness, neither shadow of turning. And the soul that finds its joy in Him alone can suffer no wavering. HANNAH WHITALL SMITH

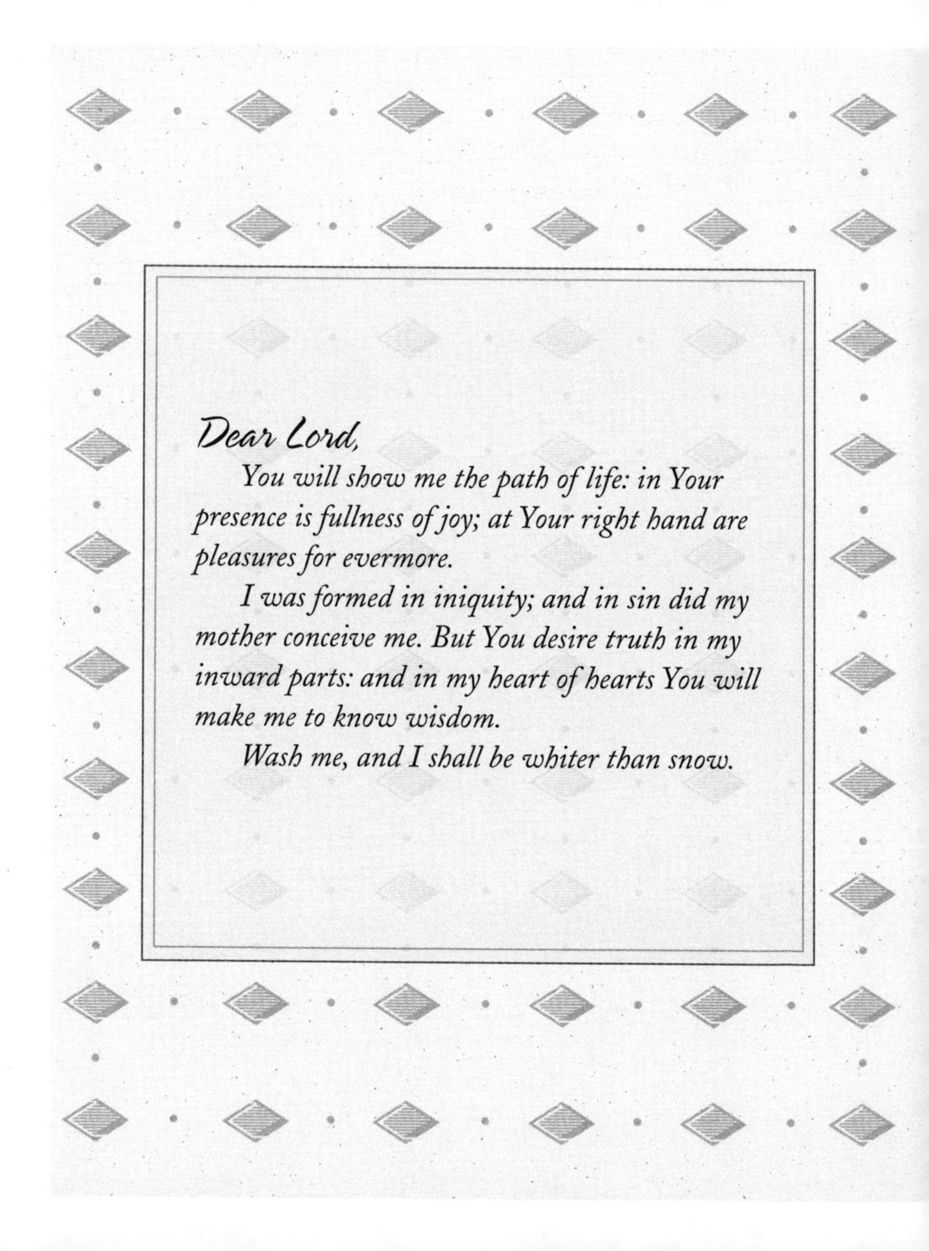

Dear Lord,

You will show me the path of life: in Your presence is fullness of joy; at Your right hand are pleasures for evermore.

I was formed in iniquity; and in sin did my mother conceive me. But You desire truth in my inward parts: and in my heart of hearts You will make me to know wisdom.

Wash me, and I shall be whiter than snow.

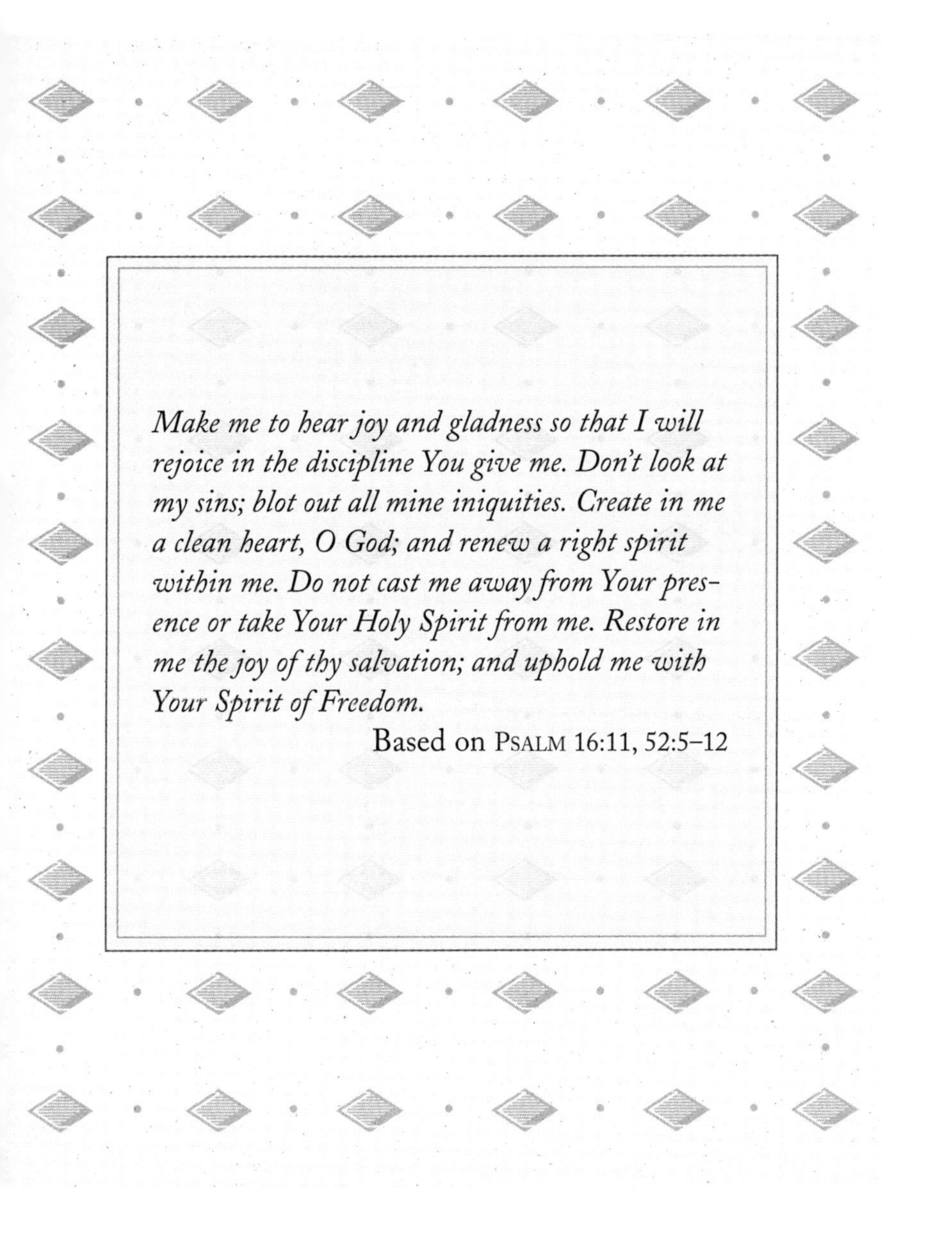

Make me to hear joy and gladness so that I will rejoice in the discipline You give me. Don't look at my sins; blot out all mine iniquities. Create in me a clean heart, O God; and renew a right spirit within me. Do not cast me away from Your presence or take Your Holy Spirit from me. Restore in me the joy of thy salvation; and uphold me with Your Spirit of Freedom.

Based on PSALM 16:11, 52:5–12

Chapter 2

Joy's Roots in the Garden of Eden

Light is sown for the righteous,
and gladness for the upright in heart.
PSALM 97:11

I thank Thee, O Lord God, that though with liberal hand Thou hast at all times showered Thy blessing upon our human kind, yet in Jesus Christ Thou hast done greater things for us than Thou ever didst before:

Making home sweeter and friends dearer:
Turning sorrow into gladness and pain into the soul's victory:
Robbing death of its sting:
Robbing sin of its power

Making peace more peaceful and joy more joyful and faith and hope more secure.
Amen. John Baillie

The Creation of Joy— And the Blight Upon It

As the faint colors of dawn glistened on the horizon, the woman stretched her perfect body on the dewy grass, luxuriating in the velvet tickle of the individual fronds beneath her. Then her eyes sprang open and she scanned the still starry sky. She could scarcely wait for dawn, for that was when God walked with her and her mate in the coolness of the day. After their twilight sleep, His warm presence dried off the night's wet chill and made their every sense come alive. He talked to them, walked with them, and showed them the secrets of this world that He created as a gift for them. Everything He made was amazing and nothing grew tiresome.

He showed them the nests woven by the robins, then the birds' sky-blue eggs, and still later, the downy hatchlings. The woman and her mate had even helped feed the hungry little ones, laughing tenderly at their open, clamoring beaks, and gently touching their small fuzzy heads while assuring the peeping young chicks that they, too, would someday soar like their parents.

God showed them the gems that grew in the hearts of the rocks, the flashing, brilliant fish in the ocean, and the scented blossoms on the fruit trees. He explained everything they wanted to know, and the woman hungrily yearned to discover more. She lapped up His knowledge in great, inexhaustible draughts. Every day was joyous, every minute a surprise.

Now, she rolled onto her side, and seeing that her mate still slept, she listened for a moment, her ears searching for God's voice on the morning air. When she heard nothing, she decided to explore on her own.

As she wandered through the gathering light, she noted that the two strange trees in the middle of the garden had gone from bloom to fruit. Although the blossoms had a heady fragrance, the fruit emitted an even more entrancing aroma. She curiously examined the fruit of the first tree.

What had God called this tree? The Tree of the Knowledge of Good and Evil, she remembered. Strange that He would forbid them its fruit. Everything else was theirs, and they were encouraged to enjoy it all—but not this.

Suddenly, Eve was aware that she was not alone. A serpent quietly glided upright toward her, and even in the dim, early morning light, the jewel-like patterns on its skin shimmered and flirted. Serpents were friendly creatures, amusing and clever, and Eve was glad for the company of this one. She stretched out her arms and it came close, its cool skin entwining about her body, seeking her warmth.

"Awaiting God?" the serpent asked, nuzzling around Eve's neck and hair, whispering in her ear.

"Oh, yes!" she breathed. "I want to ask Him more about the fruit on these two trees."

"I've heard you are not to eat from the trees in the garden," observed the serpent, his voice tinged with disapproval at the miserliness of God.

"Oh, no! We can eat of all of the trees, just not this one!" She pointed to The Tree of the Knowledge of Good and Evil. "We are not even to touch it or we will die!" she confided.

She looked curiously at the tree, wondering how something so pretty, so harmless in appearance, could possibly be deadly. She wasn't entirely sure what death actually was. She had heard God's description of death, but she had never seen it. However, she knew death was to be avoided. Whatever it was, in a world this alive, the absence of life did not seem real. She was sure death would never happen to her.

The serpent laughed and wrapped himself closer. "You won't die," he promised. "You are new to the garden, but I've been here longer and have seen much more. Let me explain to you why God is really forbidding this tree. He does not want you to eat from it because He knows something you do not know: He knows that the day you do eat from this tree, you will become as wise as He is! Your eyes will be opened! You will know good from evil! You will have His power! You will be equal with God!" The serpent paused, then hissed, "Let's keep this chat just between you and me—but if you eat from this tree, you will *be* God!"

Eve was stunned. If what the serpent said was true, she could possess all the wisdom of God! With one bite she would be like God! She would understand mysteries, such as evil and death! Exactly what was evil? Or death? Why had God withheld evil from them? Were evil and death experiences only God should enjoy? Should only He have that power when it was within her grasp to know it, too?

She studied the tree and its fruit. This was certainly not the first time she had seen it, but it was the first time she had seen it through the serpent's eyes. Here, hanging before her, the serpent said, was knowledge, power, and the ability to be like God. All this was suspended just at her fingertips, its skin tender, its smell intoxicating, and its promise of joy intriguing—hers for the taking.

She touched the fruit and found its skin strangely hot in the cool morning air. She waited for a cataclysm. Nothing happened. *The serpent was right,* she thought. *I didn't die.* She sniffed her fingertips, and her mouth began to water. She wrapped her hand around a plump specimen and gave a tug. The fruit fell in her hand.

She studied it briefly before she held it to her lips. The dawn light made the smooth skin seem so inviting. With a sigh, she sank her teeth into it.

As the juice filled her mouth, an emotion stirred within her, almost like joy—and yet oddly different. She felt cold—a strange sensation—yet queerly excited. The feeling was a little unpleasant, but novel. While she shivered in the darkness, the sweetness of the juice on her tongue invited yet another bite, so she took it. She realized the fruit was tasty but unsatisfying. She began to suspect she could eat a lot of this fruit and still be hungry. *No, that isn't possible*, she thought, so she ate more and more and more of the fruit. But the more she ate, the hungrier she felt.

A vague discomfort crept into her heart. *What is this?* she wondered. *How can I feel hunger while I am eating? How do I fill up this empty space?*

And so this is how Eve found herself severed from the True Vine. Upon her life—and ours—the moldering disease of emptiness began to grow. Whereas once she and Adam knew only pure joy, one eternal second after her teeth broke the skin of the forbidden fruit, the joy began to drain from her soul, and soon she knew sorrow, gnawing dissatisfaction, longing, shame, pain, and loneliness for God. The meat of the fruit held no joy, only the everlasting craving for it.

But God gave a promise to Eve and Adam. He promised that in another garden the snake's head would be bruised, and the seeds of eternal joy would again take root.

> *What is Christ's joy in us, but that He deigns to rejoice on our account? And what is our* joy, *which He says shall be full, but to have fellowship with Him? He had perfect joy on our account, when He rejoiced in foreknowing and predestinating us; but that joy was not in us, because we did not then exist; it began to be in us, when He called us. And this joy we rightly call our own, this joy wherewith we shall be blessed; which is begun in the faith of them who are born again, and shall be fulfilled in the reward of them who rise again.* ST. AUGUSTINE

When we are joyless, we try to manufacture joy because we know something vital is missing. We even know what is missing—joy—but it has been so long since the garden that most of us have forgotten Who created joy. We don't remember where to look for it.

Where do the saints get their joy? If we did not know some Christians well, we might think from just observing them that they have no burdens at all to bear. But we must lift the veil from our eyes. The fact that the peace, light, and joy of God is in them is proof that a burden is there as well. The burden that God places on us squeezes the grapes in our lives and produces the wine, but most of us see only the wine and not the burden. No power on earth or in hell can conquer the Spirit of God living within the human spirit; it creates an inner invincibility. OSWALD CHAMBERS

Tiny Seedlings Easily Bruised

They lay on the floor together, two little girls who were best of buddies. They had played together nicely all day, dressing the kitties in doll clothing and taking them for buggy rides, swimming in the wading pool, blowing gigantic bubbles with a special wand, and eating macaroni and cheese off a set of miniature dishes that was just right for their size. Now in their flowered summer nightgowns, they snuggled on the braided rug in front of the fireplace, their sunburned arms embracing the patient family dog that rested between them.

I was reading them a story about a make-believe boy who made funny noises. They thought the noises were very entertaining; in fact, the noises struck them as so hilarious that they went from laughing to a serious case of the giggles.

I let them chortle away for a while, and when the laughter died down a little, I asked them if I should continue. Out of the corner of her eye, one little girl looked at the other, and the giggles started all over again, this time in greater earnest than before. Each time they showed promise of subsiding, a sideways glance would begin the gales of laughter again.

Finally, both girls were so weak and exhausted from mirth that I heard barely a squeak between them. Their cheeks flushed, their breathing rhythmic, I realized that they had laughed themselves to sleep. As my husband and I carried their tired little bodies up to bed, I wondered how many times in their lives they would cry themselves to sleep. This time, at least, they had literally sailed to the Land of Nod on waves of laughter.

As a parent, I wished they could laugh themselves to sleep every night—even if it was over something as silly as the noises of a make-believe character in a book. As a fellow human being who had traveled a few miles further on life's bumpy road than they had, I sadly knew how rare the times would be that they laughed themselves to sleep.

But as these sad thoughts lingered in my mind, I couldn't

help but realize that the Heavenly Father, who created us for joy, planned from the first moment of Creation that His children would never weep in the darkness. He wanted us to laugh ourselves to sleep every night. How God must have sorrowed when disobedience entered the world! He knew that tears would then be needed to soften self-centered hearts! He knew that we would require His discipline to chop the entrenched weeds out of our lives! The Father who knows every teardrop that falls—even in the darkest of nights—knew sorrow would be necessary to produce true joy.

But it wouldn't be just our sorrow. It would be His as well.

> *It was not the pleasant things in the world that came from the devil, and the dreary things from God! It was "sin brought death into the world and all our woe"; as the sin vanishes the woe will vanish too. God Himself is the ever-blessed God. He dwells in the light of joy as well as of purity, and instead of becoming more like Him as we become more miserable, and as all the brightness and glory of life are extinguished, we become more like God as our blessedness becomes more complete. The great Christian graces are radiant with happiness. Faith, hope, charity, there is no sadness in them; and if penitence makes the heart sad, penitence belongs to the sinner, not to the saint.*
>
> ROBERT W. DALE

The Early Seeds

Your life is a joyful pilgrimage of close companionship with God, basking in His love, wisdom, and knowledge. This beautiful journey began when Jesus laid the foundations of the world, and now the ecstasy continues forever. . . .

Except that something has blocked joy's growth. Your life was supposed to travel down the Garden of Eden path! That was God's plan when He made you. He designed you—and the whole human race—to continuously experience the joy of His presence. To our sorrow, we lost that ability, but deep in our hearts we still remember. That is why we all have an insatiable and everlasting craving for joy.

> *Joy comes from seeing the complete fulfillment of the specific purpose for which I was created and born again, not from successfully doing something of my own choosing. The joy our Lord experienced came from doing what the Father sent Him to do. And He says to us, "As the Father has sent Me, I also send you"* (John 20:21 NAS).
>
> OSWALD CHAMBERS

Creation was not finished in the Garden of Eden. God is still at work, even today. But way back in the Garden of Eden, God ordained a work of creation—the restoration of human joy—that Christ finished when He came to earth. We think of the Gospels as being very different stories from the book of Genesis. But in fact, God gave the Good News to Adam and Eve all the way back in the Garden of Eden when He promised them a Savior.

Do not be afraid.
I bring you good news of great
joy that will be for all the people.
Today in the town of David
a Savior has been born to you;
He is Christ the Lord.

SPOKEN BY THE ANGEL OF
THE LORD TO SHEPHERDS,
LUKE 2:10–11 NIV

Because shadows could be deceptive on a cloudy, dark night, a sharp eye, a keen ear, and an alert mind were required to keep thieves and other predators at bay in the open field. Losses were always heavy during the winter, but this year, with the census forcing so many poor people to be on the move, the danger was magnified.

From his lookout point on the highest ridge, the shepherd's gaze endlessly swept from the horizon to the lowest folds of the valley as an unseasonably warm wind began to rise. With a practiced eye, he briefly studied the sky to determine what weather change the wind would portend.

At the moment, in the skies over Bethlehem, an oddly pulsating star caught his attention. For a fleeting moment he thought it was growing brighter. He shook his head. *A trick of the imagination,* he thought. *My eyes deceive me!* He rubbed his eyes. But when he looked again, he knew the light was growing.

He heard a strangled cry of alarm from the other shepherd on watch. Across the valley he saw his friend point fearfully at the steadily brightening beam. His frightened shriek roused the rest of the shepherds from their sleep; as one man, they sprang to their feet, mesmerized by the steadily swelling luminance.

Almost blinding in its glory, the light paused over the valley, then majestically descended into it. As it came closer, the shepherd could make out the single figure of a blazing personage. He looked like a man, but his huge stature and shimmering appearance made it clear that he was more than a mere mortal.

At the being's approach, the shepherd and his companions fell flat upon their faces in sheer terror. This entity was holy—perhaps he was God Himself!

Tumbled, terrified thoughts gripped the shepherd. *Surely I am a dead man!* his mind screamed. *I am nothing but an unimportant shepherd, a working man with dirty hands and a filthy heart. If God opens heaven to speak to one such as me, it is surely to bring judgment.*

Then the light came still nearer, sparkling, blazing, blasting off heat like a forge. Cowering with horror and shame, he thought, *In a light this pure and bright, I will die on the spot! Not even my thoughts are hidden. They betray me. I deserve nothing less than total damnation!*

As he lay quivering before the growing brilliance, the being's words rumbled across the sky and echoed off the ancient Judean hills: "Fear not!"

The shepherd could scarcely believe his ears, yet the tidings reverberated within his head and bubbled over in his heart. Perhaps he was not going to be judged on the spot and summarily dispatched to hell after all.

Then the bright stranger gave more news that cheered his heart even more: "A Savior has been born! Christ the Lord!

Here is a sign that what I am saying is true: You will find a babe wrapped in swaddling clothes, lying in a manger."

As if the initial appearance of one angelic being were not already an overwhelming assault on the senses, now every corner of the sky sprang to life with voice and light as the heavens were peeled back to reveal an uncountable legion of celestial beings. As they praised God, their words echoed the rapture felt by the shepherd to the depths of his soul: God was stepping from heaven to earth! His message was for the common laborer. And it was such good news: The shepherd had a Savior!

That night, eternal joy was born and rested in a manger.

Thou hast put gladness
in my heart,
more than in the time that
their corn and
their wine increased.

PSALM 4:7

Testimonies of Joy

We each experience a Garden of Eden moment whenever we realize our own sinfulness, and like the shepherd on that long-ago night when Christ was born, we each have a moment when God reveals to us the Good News: We have a Savior.

> *"I was very young when I accepted Christ as my Savior, but I remember being aware that I was a sinner, and I'll never forget the joy in my heart when I realized that I was forgiven and that I was going to heaven. It was like somebody opened a window and let the sunshine in!"* GRACE

> *"I had not been raised in the church, but I started to go with my girlfriend because I wanted to be with her. Every sermon seemed pointed at me! I was miserable. But after I talked with the preacher and prayed with him, my face started shining. Literally shining! I was shining on the inside, too."* LEE

> *"My aunt led me to the Lord. I was in junior high, and although I attended church, I was just waiting for someone to ask me if I knew Jesus. I was so happy that she asked me! I asked a few questions, then she prayed with me. When I opened my eyes, I was a new person because*

of the indwelling of Jesus—and I knew it. No matter what bad things have happened in my life, I've had His joy." LIZ

"A high school friend invited me to go to a party at her youth group. My family didn't go to church, but I started attending church with her and her folks. The sermons and Sunday school lessons were convicting, but I wanted to have the kind of deep-down joy my friend and her family had. One night, while riding home after church, I asked her how to ask Jesus into my heart. She told me, and after she left me off at my house, I went upstairs to my bedroom and prayed. All of a sudden, my room seemed filled with this strange light—but even more remarkable, I was filled with the Light, too! I guess it was the presence of Jesus. I had never experienced such joy." BETH

The joy for which God created us does not depend on our ability to hear an angel's song. Instead the joy woven into creation at the foundation of the world is present in all of life, no matter what our external senses tell us. Christmas comes to us on starlit, glowing winter nights—and it also comes on bleak summer days. Joy is born everywhere, every moment.

Lord, You are
my joy and happiness,
the only treasure I have
in this world.

MARGERY KEMPE

Give yourself back to Him who made you, for He is the sum of all our happiness and our perfect good. AUGUSTINE

Christmas in July

The air was so hot and humid outside it was almost too much effort to sweat. But then late July is always that way in the Illinois prairie town of Kewanee—which is one of several reasons why it was incongruent to see Mike and his sons erecting Christmas decorations on their front yard. Another reason why the display seemed so odd was that the decorations consisted of a single word: JOY—and that day the family was burying Linda, their beloved wife and mother.

The sign had done a fair piece of traveling in its life. Linda had designed it, and Mike made it when they lived in Texas. Unique and striking, the JOY sign became a landmark, first in their Texas neighborhood, then later, when they moved north, on their corner lot in Illinois.

The letters were cut from wood, brightly painted, and illuminated by floodlights, so that the message could be clearly read by pedestrians on the sidewalk or motorists on the highway. "Joy to the world!" it shouted. "Joy to all people of goodwill!"

Then the eye was drawn to the center of the O. There was the manger and its Occupant, right at the heart of JOY.

The message was clear. And now it proclaimed Linda's testimony and epitaph—and the family's hope: Jesus was the center of JOY, both in celebration and in grief, in life and in death, whether at Christmas or in July.

Because we are sinful, all of us run away from the joy God wants for us. Like Eve, we keep eating and eating the fruit that cannot satisfy, trying desperately to fill the hunger inside us. But even while we're running away, God keeps pursuing, holding out the true, nourishing fruit of joy. And when at last we turn to Him, all of heaven rejoices.

In the same way,
I tell you,
there is rejoicing in
the presence of the angels
of God over one sinner
who repents.

spoken by Jesus, LUKE 15:10 NIV

Joy Over the Returned Sinner—the View from Heaven

Around the throne they stand, the untold legions of angels, these bright beings whose created purpose is to praise and serve God. Residents of the eternal world where there is no night, no weariness, no need for sleep, they continually offer praise in the presence of their God. But occasionally, at His bidding and in response to the petitions of the saints, angels leave the throne room on special assignments to participate in the unfolding drama of salvation.

In Houston, Texas, a mother kneeling beside her bed silently beseeches God's protection over her soldier son in Korea. In heaven, God hears the prayer of her heart as though it was blasted from a trumpet. He turns to four angels. "Let no harm come to him!" commands Jehovah.

Angels quickly wing from heaven to the young man's side. They faithfully ward away dangers, most of which the young man never knew came near him.

In a ranch-style house outside Dubuque, Iowa, a man and his wife seated at their kitchen table pray about their grim financial situation. Their prayers rise before the throne in stereo harmony. God knows this couple well. He knows their faithful giving.

"Bless them," the Lord tells several angels. "Keep most of the blessings secret and unspectacular, so they will learn to look for My hand at work, but send them some surprises also. An unexpected raise in salary, too." Several flaming spirits are quickly on their way.

On a beach in the Florida Keys, a woman sits under an umbrella, squinting at the prayer list she keeps tucked in her Bible. She is on vacation, so the time away from daily pressures gives her more time to spend with the Lord. On her list is the name of a man who operates the men's shelter in Indianapolis,

Indiana. In his last prayer letter, he asked everyone to especially petition God for the salvation of an alcoholic named Troy. So she does.

All over the United States and Canada, Christian believers who received the prayer letter have been lifting Troy before the throne. Already angels have been dispatched to guide Troy to Christians who will testify about the love and delivering power of Jesus, but at this woman's prayer, more angelic reinforcements are added to the troops around him warring for his soul. However, Satan has long held captive this man's heart, and devilish troops are deeply entrenched in his life. The forces of God are losing ground.

But in the Florida Keys, the woman feels a nudging from the Holy Spirit to pray again for this young man, so she obeys. She asks that Troy be rescued from the dominion of darkness and brought into the kingdom of the Son. She prays that God would fill Troy with knowledge of His will through all spiritual wisdom. She asks that Troy come to live a life worthy of the Lord, pleasing Him in every way, bearing spiritual fruit. (Her prayer is based on Colossians 1:9-13.)

More powerful angels are dispatched to the battle for Troy's soul. Then late that afternoon, in a quiet corner of the men's shelter, the forces of heaven win a great victory: Troy prays the sinner's prayer.

Up in heaven, the throne room explodes with angelic praise.

The acclamation is not because the angelic hosts have triumphed in a long-standing war against the fallen ones of their own race, but because Troy now belongs to God. Hell is not his future; heaven is. Eternal sorrow is wiped away and replaced with eternal joy.

The angels shout: "Hallelujah! Our Lord God Almighty reigns! Let us rejoice and be glad and give Him glory." (This is their song in Revelation 19:6–7.)

God's forgiveness of humanity is a mystery to the angels. They don't really understand it. But they know the nail-scarred hands of Jesus readily hold out forgiveness to flawed, disobedient human beings. And when they take His gift, there is joy!

The Ninety and Nine

There were ninety and nine, that safely lay
In the shelter of the fold,
But one was out on the hills away,
Far off from the gates of gold—
Away on the mountains wild and bare,
Away from the tender Shepherd's care,
Away from the tender Shepherd's care.

"Lord, Thou hast here Thy ninety and nine:
Are they not enough for Thee?"
But the Shepherd made answer: "This of mine
Has wandered away from me,
And although the road be rough and steep,
I go to the desert to find my sheep,
I go to the desert to find my sheep."

But none of the ransomed ever knew
How steep were the waters crossed;
Nor how dark was the night that the Lord passed
thro'
Ere He found His sheep that was lost:
Out in the desert He heard its cry —
Sick and helpless, and ready to die,
Sick and helpless, and ready to die.

"Lord, whence are those blood drops all the way
That mark out the mountain's track?"
"They were shed for one who had gone astray
Ere the Shepherd could bring him back:"
"Lord, whence are Thy hands so rent and torn?"
"They're pierced tonight by many a thorn,
They're pierced tonight by many a thorn."

But all through the mountains, thunder-riv'n,
And up on the rocky steep,
There arose a glad cry to the gate of heaven,
"Rejoice! I have found my sheep!"
And the angels echoed around the throne,
"Rejoice! For the Lord brings back His own,
Rejoice! For the Lord brings back His own!"

ELIZABETH C. CLEPHANE

Why should the children of the King hang their heads and tote their own burdens, missing the mark about Christian victory? All this time the Holy Spirit has been wanting to make Jesus Christ our chief joy and delight!

A.W. TOZER

For too many of us, the Christian life is something of a roller-coaster ride. We painfully climb out of the pit of chastisement, enjoy an elated moment of joy in our restored relationship with God, experience prosperity, get cocky, then hurl ourselves down the tracks into sin—only to repeat the process again and again. The result is a joyless life of defeat and frustration.

Be Thou my Sun,
my selfishness destroy,
Thy atmosphere of Love be all my joy;
Thy Presence be
my sunshine ever bright,
My soul the little mote
that lives but in Thy light.

Gerhard Tersteegen

A pure heart—an honest, open soul totally without guile—belongs to the person who will find God. Many claim to be searching for God, but the person with the pure heart will have the delightful experience of finding Him. And with even more joy, she will discover God at work in the most unexpected places!

The Truth About Joy

One spring day after a sudden shower, I watched my eighteen-month-old son discover the glory and mystery of puddles. With his pudgy little hand in mine, we walked along our country blacktop road, stopping at each little lagoon of wonder. While his vocabulary was limited to necessary words like tractor, car, cookie, and no, it was plain to my observation that he believed he had uncovered something marvelous beyond his wildest hopes: He thought pieces of the sky had fallen to earth and were now within his grasp. In a sense, of course, he was right: the puddles were pieces of the sky—but not in the way he was thinking.

For him, the world was a laboratory for great experiments. Squatting down, he watched the clouds scuttle across the sky as reflected in the puddle. He squinted at the sky and then at the puddle. They looked so much alike, but he had more questions to be answered. He threw a handful of gravel into the puddle and was amazed that it disappeared. Then he threw some in the sky and was equally astonished that it clattered down around his ears. Now he knew that something was amiss with these scattered bits of heaven. He found a stick and stirred the puddle, watching the reflected sky crack into wavy pieces. Then, before I could stop him, he stepped boldly into the water, convinced that the only way to know for sure what these puddles were was to experience them for himself.

Those who are pure in heart are unafraid to ask questions about God. They step into life's puddles with total confidence. They do not fear the answers to their questions, because they want to know the Truth. The truth may not be what they expected, it may take them by surprise—but with joy they will see the One who is both the Truth and the Life!

Most of us, though, at one time or another, get our pure hearts dirtied up with selfishness. We get distracted from the true joy God wants for us, and begin to settle for artificial joys instead. But God never turns His back on us.

Joy. That's where Jesus comes in. My joy depends solely upon Him. . . . The joy of God Almighty constant and reliable and all encompassing becomes my own joy. Not bits and pieces—but full. Complete. Total.

MARABEL MORGAN

The Fruit of the Vine

The big, empty clay jugs, six of them, sat in the open air as mute witnesses of the festivities inside the house and the larger-than-expected crowd of guests. They also stood as a tribute to poor planning on somebody's part.

It was Wednesday, and Galilean weddings always took place on that day then lasted seven more, but this one was threatening to break up almost before it was started.

Jesus had observed that His mother, who was helping with the planning and execution of the feasts, was looking a little haggard. There had been a lot of whispering going on among the next-of-kin. Far more guests showed up than any of them anticipated. Who knew that the bride's family had so many relatives and that they would all show up? Not enough food! What to do? Quick! To the market to buy whatever was left from the morning's offerings! Water down the gravy and sauces, add more milk and flour, put in some extra garlic, a little pepper, and a few more onions. There! Problem solved!

Then, they had run out of the water that was used for washing hands between each meal. What to do? Haul the jugs outside. Send some of the serving girls to the city well to refill them. There! Problem solved!

Then, they had run out of wine. Now here was a shortage that could ruin everything! Too many people: not enough wine. Like the learned rabbis said, "Without wine, there is no joy!" Now this wedding was running dangerously low on both.

Quick! Send someone to the wine merchant. Bad news: No wine. Try the other wine merchant—you know, the one who sells the cheap stuff. More bad news. Now the bride is upset and her mother is crying. Could this wedding get any worse?

Mary's eye fell on her Son. In His thirty years, Jesus had always been the one this mother could count on in a pinch. When Joseph died, Jesus had stayed with her, running the carpenter's shop, acting the part of father as well as big brother until the rest of the kids were reared. No matter how bad things were, He had a solution.

"Psst! Jesus!" She called Him aside. "They have no more wine," she told Him behind her hand.

"Dear lady, why are you involving me in this? My time has not yet come," He told her. As a relative of the groom and the head of Joseph's house, He would soon be required to add His blessing on the union and present the couple with a gift, but not just yet.

Mary ignored His response. She turned to the servants. "Do whatever He says."

So now it was His turn. His mother said so. Well, honor Your father and Your mother, even if You are thirty years old and the Son of God. The Ten Commandments were to be obeyed.

The servants watched Him for instructions. "Fill the jars with water," He told them, pointing at the six large jugs. They already were hard at work at that task, running back and forth from the city well with smaller jugs and pouring the water into the bigger pots. But as soon as the pots were filled to the brim, the servants came back to Jesus and reported it.

"Draw some out and take it to the master of the feast," He told them.

They looked a little dubious, but did as they were bid.

The master of the feast was surprised to see the wine. As the one in charge of keeping the party moving, he knew a problem with supply and demand had cropped up. He also knew the usual procedure: Choice wines first: cheap wines later. *From whence had this vintage sprung?* he wondered. It was likely to be vinegary and awful. He studied the wine cautiously, curiously, swirling it about in his goblet before gaining the courage to toss his head back for a draught. His eyes grew wide with surprise.

This was good wine, very, very good wine. Where had the bridegroom found liquid ambrosia on such short notice? Surely they must have opened up someone's choice private stock.

From this very first miracle performed by Christ, we learn that there is a very good reason why Jesus is called "the Savior" and "the Redeemer:"

In our darkest moments—even the ones that are caused by our own frailties and foibles—there is One who sticks closer than a brother and who is willing to come to our rescue. He is concerned with the details of our lives—the meal that isn't right, the hairs on our head—the minutia. Just as He came to His mother's aid, He is willing to come to ours.

When our souls are as saturated with tears and sorrow in the same manner as the water that filled the clay pots to the brim, when our lives seem insipid and tasteless, He is the same Miracle Worker who can turn them into the new wine of rejoicing.

Planted Again

Although Charlie was reared in a strict but godly home, when he had the opportunity to choose for himself, he turned away from the Lord.

"I just had so many dos and don'ts at home that I didn't

want any more to do with God," said Charlie. "God wasn't anything to me but someone who disapproved of everything I wanted to do and wanted to spoil any fun I might have."

As a result, when Charlie chose a bride, he picked Dina, a woman who had absolutely no church background. They started their family and had two daughters.

God had no place in there lives, but one day Dina was introduced to a gracious, middle-aged woman named Ginny, who invited her to coffee at her home. Ginny had invited several other women, and she asked them if they would like to be part of a home Bible study. Dina knew nothing about the Bible, but she liked Ginny, and she thought it sounded interesting.

Charlie's response was immediate: "Just don't go getting religious on me! I've had more than enough of that."

Dina loved Ginny's Bible studies and fellowship time, and eventually Dina asked Jesus to be her Lord and Savior. Then Dina and Ginny both began praying for Charlie and their girls.

"At first, I wouldn't let the girls go to church with Dina," said Charlie. "I just didn't want them exposed to the Bible. But as they got into their teenage years, I realized we might need some help with them, so I thought it might be okay if they went to church. I wasn't going to go, but they could."

So Dina took the girls to church, and soon the girls also became actively involved there.

"Ginny was working on me all this time," said Charlie. "She'd see me somewhere, and she'd say in that sweet southern voice of hers, 'Charlie, you shouldn't let three beautiful women like Dina and your girls sit all alone in church! You ought to be sitting there beside them.' She was praying for me, too, and I began to think it might be a good idea for me to go to church. In fact, I thought I'd better be there!"

In time, because of the testimony of Ginny and the women in his life, as well as the exposure at church to the Word of God, Charlie yielded his life to Christ.

"I had lived in rebellion to God for so long I didn't know how unhappy I was until I asked Jesus to forgive me. All of a sudden, it was like a window opened in my soul! I knew peace and joy like I had not known since I was a child," said Charlie. "It's never left me since then. As long as I am submitting to Christ's way, I am a happy man."

This is true joy in life,
the being used for
a purpose recognized by
yourself as a mighty one.

GEORGE BERNARD SHAW

Seeds of Joyous Truth

One day as I was driving over some particularly mind-numbing back roads in rural Indiana, I listened to my kindergarten-aged son riding in the backseat sing songs he had learned at the Christian school he attended.

"O victory in Jesus," he piped in a voice pitched high enough to summon bats. "My Savior forever!" At this point, he added some lyrics to the old familiar hymn that no doubt sounded right to his young ears but were new to me: "He bopped me and socked me with His redeeming love!"

At first, I wasn't sure I had heard him correctly. "Would you sing that part again for me?" I asked, straining to hear his every word.

He sang it again, this time with even more gusto, and sure enough, my little son had Jesus "bopping and socking" him with love.

He may have technically had the lyrics wrong, but as I smiled, I realized that on several occasions Jesus had both bopped and socked me with His love. Sometimes, He needed to get my attention focused on an area of sin in my life; sometimes, He wanted me to change directions in my life; other times, He simply wanted to teach me to trust Him more.

And every time, in the end, I sang for joy!

The psalmist David understood the purpose of a song. It

unlocks the soul to expression of its deepest emotions; that's why we gravitate to the music that expresses the tune of our souls. What song does your heart sing?

> *Have the right relationship with God, finding your joy there, and out of you "will flow rivers of living water"* (John 7:38). *Be a fountain through which Jesus can pour His "living water."* OSWALD CHAMBERS

For our heart shall
rejoice in him,
because we have trusted
in his holy name.

PSALM 33:21

A Prayer of Thanksgiving

Gratitude for the Joy That Was Promised in the Garden of Eden

My soul glorifies the Lord and my spirit rejoices in God my Savior, for He has been mindful of the humble state of His servant. The Mighty One has done great things for me—Holy is His name.

His mercy extends to those who fear Him, from generation to generation. He has performed mighty deeds with His arm; He has scattered those who are proud in their inmost thoughts.

He has brought down rulers from their thrones but has lifted up the humble. He has filled the hungry with good things but sent the rich away empty.

He has sent us Christ.

Based on LUKE 1:46–53

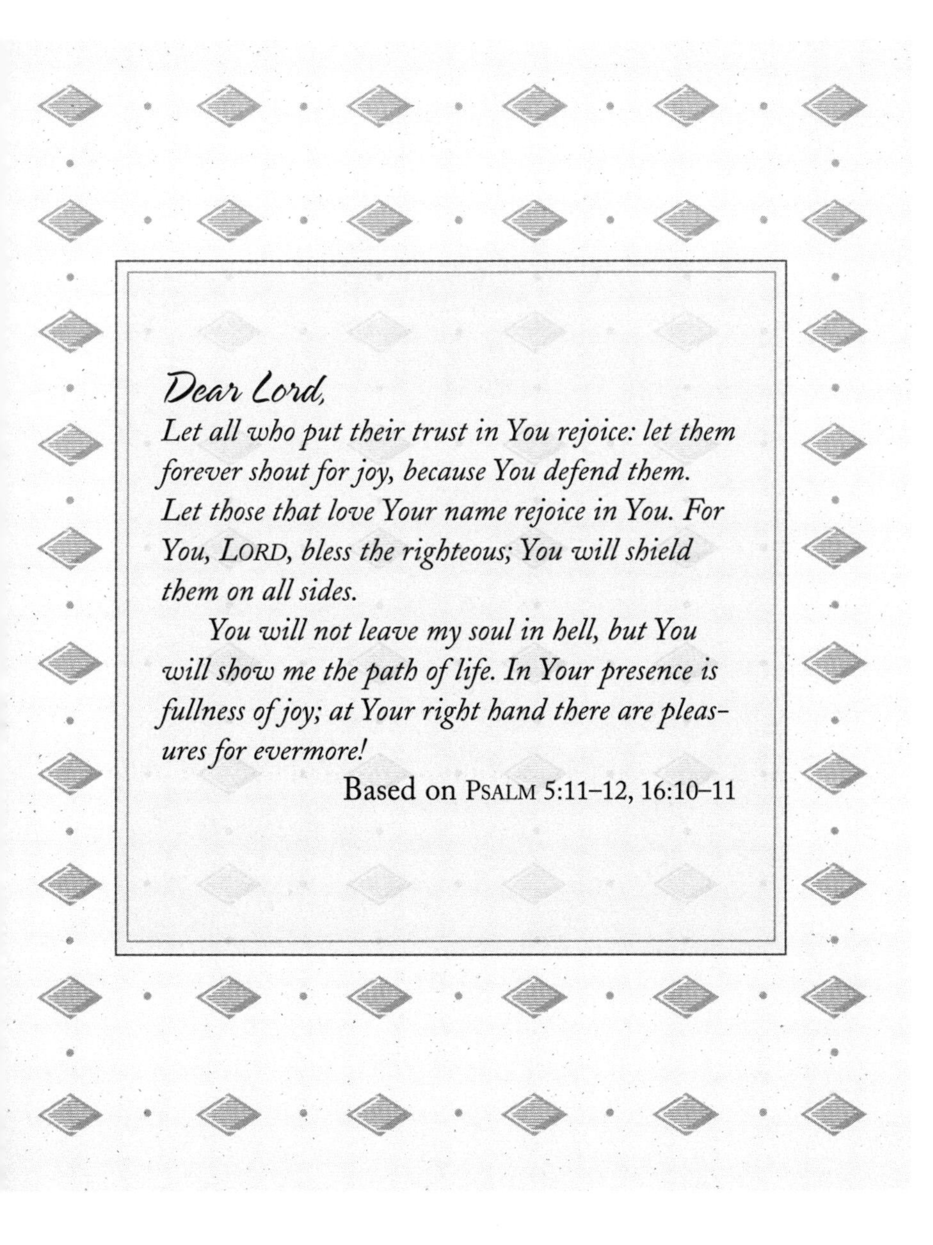

Dear Lord,

Let all who put their trust in You rejoice: let them forever shout for joy, because You defend them. Let those that love Your name rejoice in You. For You, LORD, bless the righteous; You will shield them on all sides.

You will not leave my soul in hell, but You will show me the path of life. In Your presence is fullness of joy; at Your right hand there are pleasures for evermore!

Based on PSALM 5:11–12, 16:10–11

Chapter 3

Grafting onto the Vine:
Opening Our Hearts to the Spirit's Joy

Though now ye see him not, yet believing,
ye rejoice with joy unspeakable
and full of glory.
1 PETER 1:8

The joy that Jesus gives is
the result of our disposition being
at one with His own disposition.

OSWALD CHAMBERS

Resurrected Joy

Although the scorching sun beat mercilessly on the limestone caves, the man leaned against them totally unaware of the burning damage it was doing to his skin. His body was numb to all pain because his soul was racked and tortured. He pressed his ear against the wall and listened.

Silence within the cave. This was a good sign, he believed. His beloved still slept. He had time to rescue the body from the cave and take it home.

His mind could not accept that his loved one was dead. With his own eyes he had seen the body shift from warm to cold, soft to stiff, alive to forever asleep. But his mind did not believe his eyes. They lied. He simply would not believe them.

How long he'd sat in his house, staring, and guarding the body no one knew. Eventually, neighbors noticed the bad smell, came to investigate, and found them. Then they started meddling. Embalmers, mourners, family, friends—they were all wrong. Beloved was not dead; only resting. "At night, my dear one rises up and speaks to me!" he told them. "The body is only dead during the daytime. At night, it lives!" They didn't believe him: They looked sad, patted his shoulder—some even wailed and cried.

"Go away! Let us alone!" he told them, but they would not. "This is a hot climate," they said. They insisted on wrapping the body with spices and put it in these caves. They put a heavy stone over the cave door and restrained him while he screamed "No! No!" and tore his clothing. Now that they were gone away, he'd move the stone, and they would be together once more. He would take his precious one home.

It had required several men to roll the stone down the hill and over the cave door, but it demanded only one anguished soul to shift it enough to gain entry. Once ajar, the cave exhaled the cool, rancid breath of the captives. The man was oblivious to the smell; he didn't even sniff. The shaft of sunlight only pierced in a short distance so the man began to desperately flail around with his arms, bruising them against the walls, disturbing dust and bones.

Finally, he found a putrid, rag-wrapped bundle. He gathered it into his arms and ran to the light. He tore layer after layer of fabric off of the head. He came closer and closer to the face, found the final wrap, then triumphantly ripped it free. As if part of a hilarious, cosmic joke, the skull grinned at him briefly before falling backwards off the spine, shattering on the cave floor. He roared in anger and threw the corpse remnant against the wall.

He charged back into the cave. Now even the dead were conspiring against him to take away his loved one! It would not happen! He would break every bone! He would destroy every carcass. The living had hidden his precious one and the cadavers were their allies. He would fight them all! Body after body was torn from its resting place, thrust into the daylight, its face searched for answers, and when they gave none, cast down on the rocks below and broken. Where was his loved one? He could hear the familiar voice begging him for help, then accusing him of desertion. "I'm coming! I'm sorry!" he cried as he rifled the caves, but the voice continued to speak. Then it was joined by others.

Back in the village, the city fathers called an emergency meeting with the man's family. Day and night, his screams echoed through the graves and in the city streets. He had to be contained, the bones put back, and restitution paid for the damage. A brave delegation went to the cemetery to try to talk some reason into him, but retreated under a volley of rocks and skulls. Finally, a platoon of professional soldiers cornered him. He meekly allowed them to chain him to the prison wall. The next morning, he was gone, the chains stretched and snapped.

"A fluke," they said, "something wrong with the chains." So they tried again.

And again. And again with the same results.

After that, people stayed away from that section of the Galilee coast.

They buried their dead in other caves. Occasionally, a boat or a ship would land on the beach beneath the cliffs only to be confronted by a raving, naked, bloody man with the remnants of manacles hanging from his wrists. The only one bold enough to approach the area was a hog farmer who staked his herd on the plain within sight of the caves. It was a hazardous place; no one else wanted it. Now and again, a hog carcass would turn up, bloody and savaged as if someone had gnawed on its raw meat. The herdsman charged it off to overhead.

Then Jesus' boat pulled near the shore. A couple of the disciples leaped into the surf, mooring ropes in hand, and towed the boat up onto the beach. As soon as His foot touched the sand, the unkempt, wild head of the lunatic appeared over the edge of the cliffs. His screams echoed and rang off the rocks below.

"What are You doing here, Jesus, Son of the Most High God? Have You come to send me to hell before my time? I beg You, in God's name, do not torture me!"

As the disciples watched from down below, Jesus began climbing the cliff, picking His way among the rocks to the man's side. As He reached out to touch him, the man shrieked fearfully, as if flames of fire were shooting out of Jesus' hand.

"What is your name, you unclean spirit?" Jesus asked.

The man thrust his face into Jesus' and his voice roared like an attacking horde, "My name is Legion, for we are many!" Then he wilted and fell to the ground. "Please!" the voices begged, "do not send us out of this land! Do not send us to hell before our time! Send us into the pigs!"

Jesus looked across the plateau. He saw the huge herd, about two thousand pigs, peaceably rooting the ground, searching for tasty morsels.

"Go!" Jesus commanded. The man rolled on the ground heaving with convulsing wrenches. Within an instant, the pigs startled. Wild-eyed and frenzied, they ran for cliffs, hurling themselves over into the sea.

Waves upon wave, they fell, squealing, flailing, crying. The herdsmen ran after them, shouting "Stop! Stop!" to no avail. They stood at the edge of the cliff watching the sea boil with swine intent upon drowning themselves. Their eyes filled with fear as they saw the former wild man sobbing and clinging to the feet of Jesus.

Regardless of the identity of the demons who had plagued him for so long, he was now a man in his right mind. The demons' death-grip had been shaken loose. Although his body was still filthy with the residue of their domination, his soul was clean. His loved one's death was now understood as a part of life. Although sorrow had corrupted his life, joy in Jesus would bring resurrection. (Based on Mark 5.)

Joy is planted in our lives when we open our hearts to the same joy promised in the Garden of Eden, the joy revealed to the shepherds centuries later on that first Christmas night. But if our joy is to grow strong, if it is to blossom and bear fruit, we cannot hope to produce it by our own strength. Joy's growth is dependent on the Holy Spirit. We must be grafted onto His life-giving vine.

Is your life joyless and flat? Do you feel imprisoned by the circumstances in your life? Are you caged by your own inadequacies, fears, illnesses, or state of affairs? Then it is time to let the Holy Spirit open the bars that entrap your soul and give you joy!

There are many joys in life—the joys most people encounter frequently—and then there is supernaturally inspired joy that only comes from the grafting of our souls onto the vine of the Holy Spirit.

> *When I have really transacted business with God on the basis of His covenant, letting everything else go, there is no sense of personal achievement—no human ingredient in it at all. Instead, there is a complete overwhelming sense of being brought into union with God, and my life is transformed and radiates peace and joy.*
>
> OSWALD CHAMBERS

You cannot artificially grow God's joy. You cannot manufacture it. It is implanted in your soul by the Supernatural Seed of God, nurtured by the warmth of His Spirit, pruned by His loving hands, and brought to glorious fruition by the miracle of His constant presence.

> *The undiminished radiance, which is the result of the abundant joy, is not built on anything passing, but on the love of God that nothing can change. And the experiences of life, whether they are everyday events or terrifying ones, are powerless to "separate us from the love of God which is in Christ Jesus our Lord"* (Romans 8:39).
>
> OSWALD CHAMBERS

As Christians, we must bring every thought under the discipline of the Holy Spirit. Disobedience—even if it is not acted upon, even if you think no one knows—can make you stumble in your walk with God and your relationships with others. Disobedience and rebellion in the mind is the biggest thief of joy. It's what comes between us and the Holy Spirit.

The way to enjoy indestructible. . .joy is to determine:

> *1. To do whatever God commands, however difficult.*
> *2. To endure whatever God appoints, however severe.*
> *3. To obtain whatever God promises, however unattainable.*
> *4. To die daily, however costly the crucifixion.*
> *5. To love my "enemies," however misunderstood in this.*
> *6. To pray without ceasing, and in everything give thanks.*

This will give one a healthy soul. . . .
Otherwise, we may cry with Joel:
"Joy is withered away. . . .
Is not the meat cut off before
our eyes, yea, joy and gladness
from the house of our God?"

(FROM JOEL 1:12, 16)
LEONARD RAVENHILL

Planting the Seed of Joy Incarnate in Your Soul

The same Holy Spirit who planted the Seed of God in the womb of Mary is the same Holy Spirit who plants the Seed of God in your heart. The fruit of Mary's womb was Joy Incarnate in the Person of Jesus. The fruit of your heart can be Joy Eternal in the Person of Jesus. To implant this Joy, God only waits to hear from your lips the same words spoken by Mary: "I am the Lord's servant. May it be to me as You have said." (Paraphrase of Luke 1:38.)

The heart overflows with gladness,
and leaps and dances for
the joy it has found in God.
In this experience
the Holy Spirit is active,
and has taught us in the flash of a
moment the deep secret of joy.
You will have as much joy
and laughter in life as you have
faith in God.

MARTIN LUTHER

A Prayer That Brings the Holy Spirit's Joy

Dear Lord,
Have mercy on me according to Your loving-kindness. According to the multitude of Your tender mercies, blot out my crimes. Wash me thoroughly from my iniquity. Cleanse me from my sin.

I freely admit the crimes I've committed against You, and I am always reminded of my sin. Against You and only You have I sinned! I was sinful before I was even born!

You desire me to understand the truth and not to hide even from myself. Wash me, purge me, and I shall be whiter than snow. Make me joyous and glad even over the parts of my life that seem broken now.

Blot out my sins. Create a clean heart in me, O God, and renew a right spirit within me. Do not cast me away from Your presence or take Your Holy Spirit from me.

Restore unto me the joy of Your salvation.

Based on Psalm 51:1–12

What was the joy that Jesus had? Joy should not be confused with happiness. . . . The joy of Jesus was His absolute self-surrender and self-sacrifice to His Father—the joy of doing that which the Father sent Him to do. . . . Jesus prayed that our joy might continue fulfilling itself until it becomes the same joy as His. . . . Living a full and overflowing life does not rest in bodily health, in circumstances, nor even in seeing God's work succeed, but in the perfect understanding of God, and in the same fellowship and oneness with Him that Jesus Himself enjoyed. But the first thing that will hinder this joy is the subtle irritability caused by giving too much thought to our circumstances. Jesus said, ". . .the cares of this world, . . .choke the word, and it becomes unfruitful" (Mark 4:19). . . . Have the right relationship with God, finding your joy there, and out of you "will flow rivers of living water" (John 7:38).

OSWALD CHAMBERS

One Way to Open Our Hearts to the Spirit's Sustenance

In the wee dawn hours when the rest of the house was asleep, high school junior Ashley awakens, creeps downstairs to the furnace room with her Bible, and spends time alone with the Lord.

"I go down to the furnace room because I share a room with my sister and I know she'd resent it if I turned on the lights to read my Bible," said Ashley. "Also, I think I'd feel a little self-conscious praying with her in the room. Besides, it's warm down there and if I stayed in bed, I'd probably go back to sleep!"

Ashley was familiar with the Bible, its verses and stories, but when she read them for herself, her relationship with God underwent a big change. "I've been in church since I was little girl, and my parents had family devotions with me when I was younger. I enjoyed the Bible, but it wasn't until I started reading it for myself that it became my delight!" said Ashley.

She described her study technique. "I always start with prayer. I ask God to send the Holy Spirit to reveal to me the meaning of the passages. When I read a section, I study it with the expectation that God is going to open my eyes to a new truth, and I'm never disappointed. What amazes me is that although I think I know a chapter or a verse pretty well, all of a sudden some new thought will appear in my head. I guess that is why they call the Bible the 'Living Word.'

"In John 1, the passage explains how the Word was in the beginning, how it was with God, and was God. Now, in Christ, the Word is made flesh (John 1:1, 4). When I read a passage, I 'see' Jesus saying the words to me. When I don't understand something, I ask Him for explanation. I believe His Spirit does just that."

> *I still constantly find that when I am without the Word, Christ is gone, yes, and so are joy and the Spirit. But as soon as I look at the Psalms or a passage of Scripture, it so shines and burns into my heart that I gain a different spirit and mind.* MARTIN LUTHER

Our lives will be joyful so long as we are connected to the source of all true joy: the Spirit of God. Without Him, this fruit of the Spirit will shrivel and die in our lives.

> *Joy was characteristic of the Christian community so long as it was growing, expanding, creating healthfully. The time came when the Church had ceased to grow, except externally in wealth, power, and prestige; and these are mere outward adornments, or hampering burdens, very likely. They do not imply growth or creativeness. The time came when dogmatism, tyranny, and ignorance strangled the free intellectual activity of the Church, and worldliness*

destroyed its moral fruitfulness. Then joy spread her wings and flew away. The Christian graces care nothing for names and labels; where the Spirit of the Lord is, there they abide, but not in great Churches that have forgotten Him. How little of joy there is in the character of the religious bigot or fanatic, or in the prudent ecclesiastical statesman! A show of cheerfulness they may cultivate, as they often do; but it is like the crackling of thorns under a pot: we cannot mistake it for the joy of the Lord which is the strength of the true Christian.

WILLIAM R. INGE, *Personal Religion*

Nourishing Your Soul in the Spirit

Like water on a parched ground, the Word of God is just what your soul desires. Some people say, "I can't understand the Bible. It doesn't do me any good to read it." To them, I suggest that they not merely read the Bible, but memorize it. Choose a short verse and repeat it over and over and over and over until it sticks in your brain. Write it down, maybe ten times. Keep it on a three-by-five card on your visor, shaving mirror, computer desk, next to your sink, wherever you perform those daily mindless tasks. Ask the Holy Spirit to teach you the verse. You will be surprised at what He shows you. The Word of God is living and powerful; the Holy Spirit will show you from each verse the truths you need for your life, and as He does so, you will find His life flowing into you more and more.

We cannot have joy unless we open ourselves to the Word. And joy will not flourish in our lives unless we are surrendered to the Spirit.

"We will never know the joy of self-sacrifice until we surrender in every detail of our lives. Yet self-surrender is the most difficult thing for us to do. We make it conditional by saying, 'I'll surrender if. . . !' Or we approach it by saying, 'I suppose I have to devote my life to God.' We will never find the joy of self-sacrifice in either of these ways.

But as soon as we do totally surrender, abandoning ourselves to Jesus, the Holy Spirit gives us a taste of His joy. The ultimate goal of self-sacrifice is to lay down our lives for our Friend (John 15:13-14). When the Holy Spirit comes into our lives, our greatest desire is to lay down our lives for Jesus. Yet the thought of self-sacrifice never even crosses our minds, because sacrifice is the Holy Spirit's ultimate expression of love.

OSWALD CHAMBERS

Joy Journal—
A Record of Your Growth

It only takes a minute, but what great dividends it pays to keep a Joy Journal! All you need is a blank book or notebook and a pencil. You will find this a wonderful prelude to your prayer and praise time with the Lord, plus a lasting reminder of His goodness.

Just before you begin your daily prayer time, under the date, jot down the blessings you have received from the Lord. Try to think of at least seven each day. Add the life lessons you have been taught by the Holy Spirit. It will give you a record of what God has done for you—and it will leave a witness to your family and future generations of the joy in knowing Jesus.

Now the God of hope fill you
with all joy and peace in believing,
that ye may abound in hope,
through the power of the Holy Ghost.

ROMANS 15:13

There is joyous music in the soul that is filled with the Holy Spirit! The central theme of each song is Jesus. Joy inspired by the Holy Spirit rejoices in what Christ has done and will do for us, not what we have done or will do for Him.

The kingdom of God
is not meat and drink;
but righteousness, and peace,
and joy in the Holy Ghost.

ROMANS 14:17

Be filled with the Spirit; Speaking to yourselves in psalms and hymns and spiritual songs, singing and making melody in your heart to the Lord.

EPHESIANS 5:18–19

And the disciples were
filled with joy,
and with the Holy Ghost.

ACTS 13:52

Joy as sparked by the Holy Spirit is never selfish. It does not insist on just pleasing ourselves, but in bringing joy to others, too. If our joy brought wounds, sorrow, or sin to another, our joy would turn to grief for us.

What are the "how-to's" for an effective spiritual life? Are there daily practices that Christians should pursue?

- *A daily life of praise, thanksgiving, and adoration of God.*
- *A daily life of prayer, fellowship, and a communion with God.*
- *A daily life of love, a delight in the personal assurance of God's love and a desire to share His love with others.*

KENNETH W. OSBECK

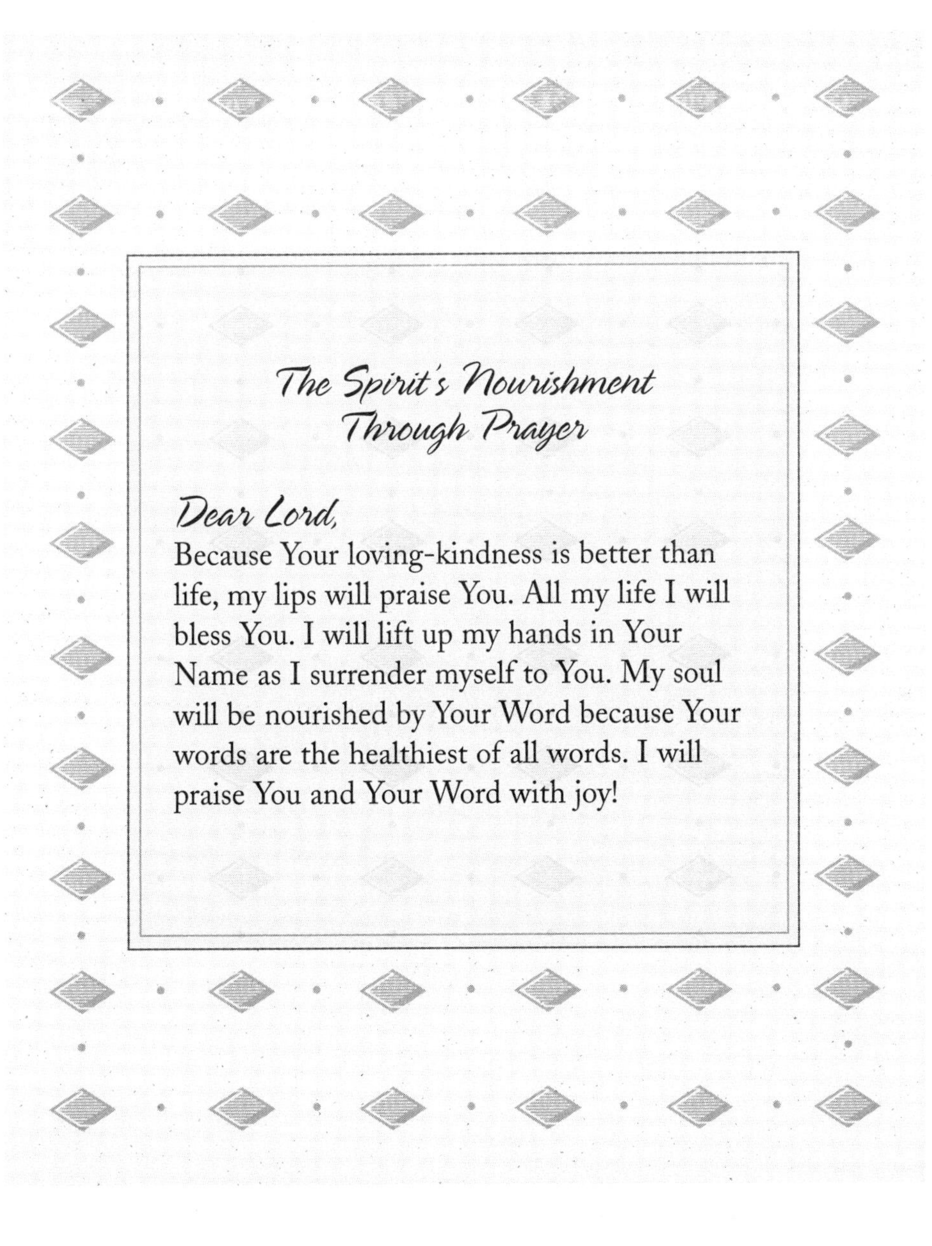

The Spirit's Nourishment Through Prayer

Dear Lord,

Because Your loving-kindness is better than life, my lips will praise You. All my life I will bless You. I will lift up my hands in Your Name as I surrender myself to You. My soul will be nourished by Your Word because Your words are the healthiest of all words. I will praise You and Your Word with joy!

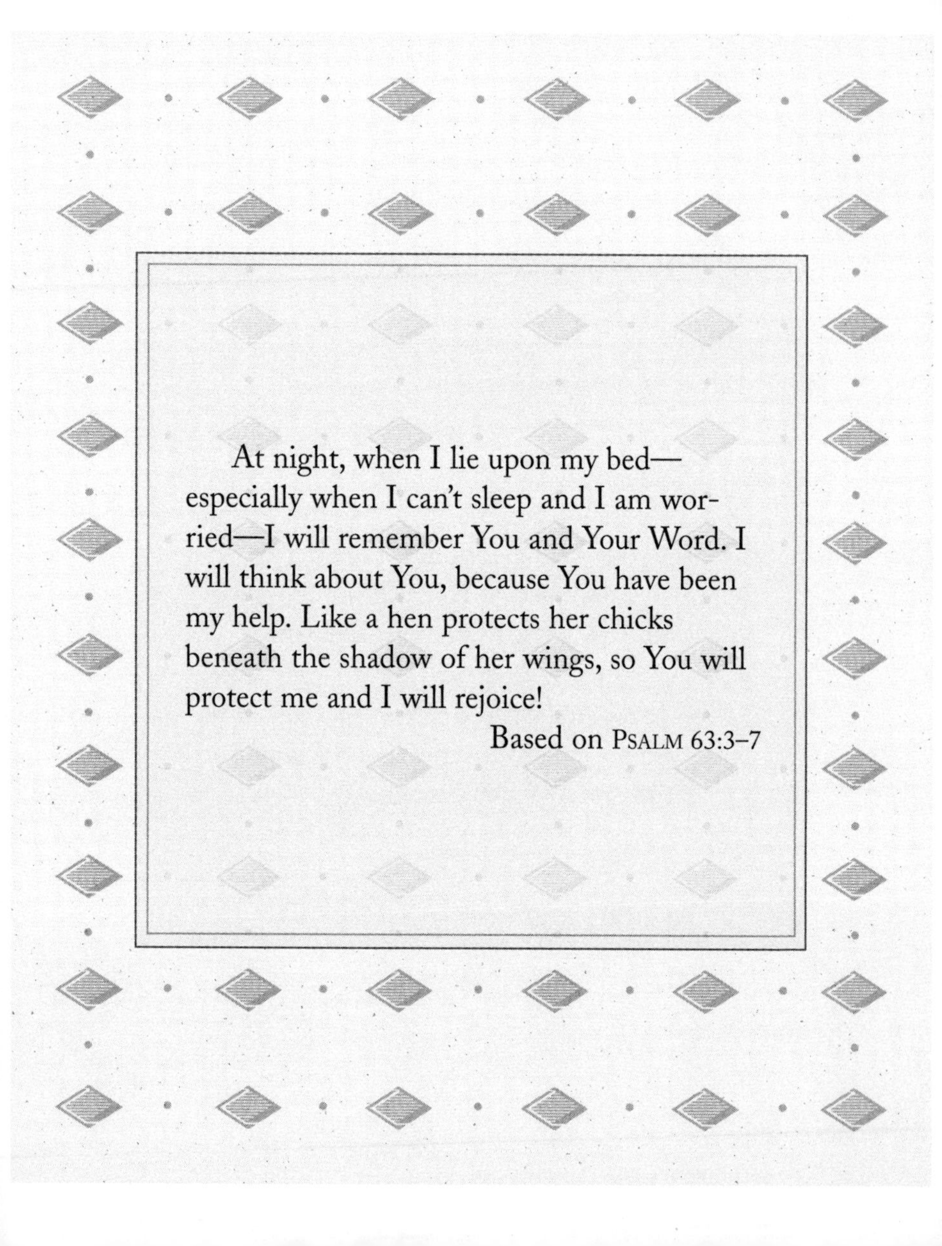

At night, when I lie upon my bed—especially when I can't sleep and I am worried—I will remember You and Your Word. I will think about You, because You have been my help. Like a hen protects her chicks beneath the shadow of her wings, so You will protect me and I will rejoice!

Based on PSALM 63:3–7

Chapter 4

Propagating the Roots of Joy

I will rejoice in the Lord,
I will joy in the God
of my salvation.

HABAKKUK 3:18

Joy is the characteristic by which God uses us to remake the distressing into the desired, the discarded into the creative. Joy is prayer—Joy is strength—Joy is love—Joy is a net of love by which we can catch souls. MOTHER TERESA

Once we have found the joy of Christ, once we have opened our hearts to the Spirit's daily sustenance, then it is only natural we would want to spread this joy we've found to those around us. This chapter will give you some ideas on how to propagate joy's roots—to your families, to your neighbors, to strangers. We are called to offer the joy of Christ to a hungry world.

Homegrown Joy—
Make a Memory Book of Joy

This is a good way to spread joy within your own family. Make a scrapbook with photos illustrating the joys and blessings God has given you or your family. It's a wonderful activity to do with children—and the final product is a marvelous gift for very young ones. They'll enjoy looking at it over and over again, and it will help cement in their minds the way God loves them as individuals.

Sort through photos for pictures of grandparents, relatives, houses, fun activities, seasonal celebrations, and special events, such as a new tooth or a Boy Scout award. (You might want to use your "seconds" or photos that aren't the best exposures, or your double prints.) Organize the photos by subjects, such as

Family, Friends, Blessings, Ways We Celebrate Jesus, Special Moments, etc.

Using an expandable scrapbook or photo album, insert the prints to illustrate each heading. For example, on the pages in the Family section, you might have photos of grandparents, Dad with the kids, each of the children, Mom, aunts, uncles, or cousins. Under each photo, add a label explaining why each person is a joyous blessing from God. If you are working with children, let them tell you why each person is a gift from God. You'll enjoy their answers now and in years to come.

As your children grow, encourage them to add pages and sections to their albums. These also make great gifts for children to give at Christmas.

Parents can make albums like these for each of their children and entitle them: Why I Thank God for [Child's Name]. Adopted children especially find this type of album healing and helpful.

> *Blessed is the people that know the joyful sound: they shall walk, O* L*ORD, in the light of thy countenance. In thy name shall they rejoice all the day: and in thy righteousness shall they be exalted.* PSALM 89:15–16

One of the great secrets of happiness is to think of happy things. There were many unhappy things in Philippi. . . . The Christians of that town might easily have had their lives stained by continually letting their thoughts dwell on what they could not help seeing and hearing and feeling. . . .

But they were definitely told to think of things true, honorable, just, pure, lovely, and of good report.

AMY CARMICHAEL

More Homegrown Joy

When Jim's work took him long distances from home, Jody had to become both mother and father to the couple's three preschool children.

"He didn't want to be gone, and he really missed me and the kids, but until something opened up where we could be together, he would sometimes have to be gone for a month or more at a time," said Jody. "He usually got home for birthdays and holidays; but one year, the company sent him overseas, and he couldn't come home for Christmas."

The children were just at the age where they could remember what Christmas was all about. "They loved the manger scene with Baby Jesus in it, and the lights, and the tree. They were just excited about everything—but most of all, they were looking forward to their daddy coming home. I kept hoping that something would happen, and he would be able to be there, but about the middle of December, I realized it just wasn't going to be," said Jody.

That was when Jody decided to distract the children's attention from Daddy coming home for their Christmas and start focusing it on making Christmas for Daddy far away.

"I knew we couldn't send too much in the way of presents, so I thought and prayed about what would be meaningful to Jim," said Jody. "When the kids were practicing for the pageant at church, it dawned on me what to do."

Jody borrowed a movie camera, and while her children acted out the Christmas story, she taped them. "It was really cute! Our eighteen-month-old played the part of Baby Jesus, and he kept getting out of the manger—a laundry basket—and running away. 'Mary' had to catch him and try to get him to lay down. At one point, the manger tipped completely over with Baby Jesus under it, so Mary just sat on it to keep him corralled!"

But Jody thought of an even better gift for Jim. "I had each of the children tell me what they liked about their daddy while I typed their replies, about ten answers each. I asked them to remember something fun they did with their daddy and tell me about it. I was surprised by what was special to the kids—

and I think Jim was, too, when he read them."

Jody cut each reply into an individual strip, and let the kids decorate the strips with stickers and crayons before folding them up into a little box they sent to Jim.

Among the children's replies: "I like it when Daddy gives me whisker rubs and says, 'You're my boy, aren't you?' " "I liked it when Daddy let me put my name on the [fresh cement work on the] sidewalk." "At the baseball game Daddy got me candy and all that. He also bought me pop. I liked the pop." "Daddy is strong and tall. If I'm lost and I find Daddy, I want to hold him really tight." "I like it when he wrestles and plays." And so forth. The children's thoughts brought tears to their parents' eyes.

"It has been many years since we made that Christmas gift," Jody said, "and although the older kids are in college now, Jim has always kept it. He says it is the best Christmas gift he ever received. That was a hard Christmas, having Jim gone—but I guess real joy depends more on love than anything else."

No man truly has joy
unless he lives in love.

THOMAS AQUINAS

During a trip to the grocery store, Liz spotted a notation on the cash register. It read: "Do not accept any more checks from Bill Bailey."

"I knew Bill and his wife," said Liz, "from the time we were children together, and I also knew that they were having some real financial troubles on their farm just then. So I called the store manager aside and asked him about the note. I guess he shouldn't have told me anything, but this was a small town, and people loved to gossip. He told me Bill had bounced a check for about twenty dollars and that Bill had said he just couldn't make it good because he didn't have any money.

"Without going into a lot of detail, I told the manager about Bill's problems, and asked if he would remove the sign if I paid off Bill's check. He agreed, so I paid it off."

Liz said she started thinking about all the farm families she knew that were having financial trouble just then. "It was getting close to Christmas, and I knew another neighbor was facing bankruptcy. There probably wouldn't be any celebrating at their house," said Liz. "My children went to school with this neighbor's kids, and they said the kids often cried on the bus and playground because they were worried about their parents losing the farm. I gathered our family together and said, 'Okay, let's pray about what we should do to help this family.'

"We prayed, and afterward our youngest said, 'I think we should make and sell homemade candy!' I had made some rock candy earlier in the week, and the kids thought it was the best ever.

"So we tried it. I made another batch of candy, colored and flavored it, and poured it into some novelty candy molds. The kids took it to school and sold everything. This went on day after day, until we raised over a hundred dollars. We had a lot of fun making the candy, and the kids enjoyed selling it. But what was really fun was anticipating the surprise this family was going to feel when they found they had received a special, anonymous Christmas gift.

"I took the money down to our local grocer and asked him to call our neighbors. He told them that a friend had bought them one hundred and twenty-five dollars' worth of groceries and that they should come down and pick them out. He didn't tell them who it was, only that they should accept the gift as from the hand of the Lord. I made sure he added that when they got on their feet again, they should pass the gift on to others.

"A few days later, the grocer took me aside and said the husband and wife both started crying when he told them about the gift. But I think we probably got more joy out of that gift than they did!"

The Odor of Blessing

Be imitators of God, therefore, as dearly loved children and live a life of love, just as Christ loved us and gave himself up for us as a fragrant offering and sacrifice to God. EPHESIANS 5:1–2 NIV

Brother and Sister Nugent smelled of cattle disinfectant. It was almost overwhelming. Nothing, absolutely nothing—not Aqua Velva, Avon perfume, nor Watkins Apple Blossom toilet water—covered its pungent, make-your-eyes-water odor.

The Nugents had a big cattle operation, and with the aid of their bachelor son, Clete, they milked about one hundred and fifty head of cattle.

They used the disinfectant to sterilize their cows, equipment, and apparently themselves.

Actually, they must have steeped themselves in it, for the smell of it seemed to ooze out from their pores. Wafts of it eddied around them as they moved; little fragrant traces remained wherever they had been.

Brother Nugent was a large, strong specimen of a corn-fed plowboy, but Sister Nugent was a really big woman, and I think she could have taken him in a fair fight. She rocked from side-to-side when she walked, rather like she was carrying a small steer under each arm and a bale of hay in each hand. She probably could have done it, too.

Like many long-married couples, the Nugents looked alike. Both had big, full-moon, smiling, freckled faces—and whiskers. Brother Nugent seemed to have trouble mowing his off, so not infrequently, little patches of bristles remained like weeds growing around fence posts. Sister Nugent also had an impressive collection of stiff, gray and white bristles that grew straight out from her chin and upper lip. When she moved in for a kiss, there was no way to avoid being stabbed by them.

This friendly, malodorous couple loved little children. Since their own kids—with the exception of Clete—were all grown up and moved away, they liberally commandeered hugs and kisses off of us church kids.

Neither of them seemed to know their own strength, and so being loved by either Brother or Sister Nugent was like being put through a washing machine wringer while simultaneously being scrubbed with a wire brush.

"Give Gramma Nugent a hug and a little sugar," Sister Nugent would say to a small, hapless victim. So with nose wrinkled against the stinging olfactory assault of disinfectant, we children would open our arms to a rib-crushing hug, coupled with a prickly kiss, and receive a piece of candy in return.

Sometimes it was wrapped; but mostly, it was pretty pieces of striped Christmas candy or pink wintergreen lozenges, the kind that taste like liniment. Sister Nugent was tidy, so the candy she gave us didn't have extra bits of lint and threads attached, but it did have a distinctive odor and taste—cattle disinfectant.

A child only had to be mashed to jelly, punctured, and given the Nugent's distinctively-flavored candy to know for all eternity that it was an experience to be avoided if at all humanly possible. The older kids were good at getting away, but younger children, the ones who weren't fast enough to escape, were routinely caught, squished, and perforated.

Brother and Sister Nugent loved to give, not just disinfectant-flavored candy and whiskery kisses, but food and money and just about anything else they had in their big, callused hands.

Missionaries passing the offering plate found their needs met with crisp, indelicately-scented one hundred dollar bills. Out-of-work folks discovered their grocery bills had been paid and that they had a mysterious credit balance which dried up just as they found work. No one in the congregation could be sick without finding a crumb-topped casserole on their doorstep keeping company with a big, yeasty loaf of homemade bread, Nugent-flavored—all bounty from their generous hearts and hands.

As beauty is in the eye of the beholder, so fragrance is in the nose of the sniffer.

As a pastor, my father believed that if he was going to preach about faith in God, he should practice it in his own life. Consequently, even though he was the father of eight children, he did not receive a regular salary. Instead, a faith offering was collected each week. Whatever came in that offering was what God provided and we lived on that.

However, sometimes, it just wasn't enough.

We had a policy and practice in our home of taking additional needs to the Lord in prayer. In family devotions, the need would be mentioned, and with one voice—pitched higher or lower—we would pray for God to supply it. The need wasn't to be mentioned to anyone outside the family circle or the throne room of God, so that when the answer came, we knew it came from the Lord.

I can't remember anymore exactly what our need was, but it had something to do with money. More specifically, the lack of money. As was our practice, the family lifted the need before the Lord—and waited.

Not long afterwards, the answer came in an anonymous envelope, strongly scented with a pungent odor.

"Whew!" somebody said, "That envelope smells like the Nugents! It really stinks!"

"Take a good whiff," said Dad. "That's what an answer to prayer smells like."

It was also the smell of faithful, sacrificial love.

Here is the truly Christian life, here is faith really working by love: when a man applies himself with joy and love to the works of that freest servitude, in which he serves others voluntarily and for naught; himself abundantly satisfied in the fulness and richness of his own faith.

MARTIN LUTHER

Pass the Blessing, Please!

I want to launch a new national holiday: Blessing Day. It could be planned for sometime in midwinter, when there aren't any holidays, and all of us need a little cheering up. Blessing Day would be a time when we remember the people God has used to encourage, teach, and help us grow spiritually. It would be a day when we say a hearty and heartfelt thank-you to the individuals who have labored to introduce us to real joy.

On Blessing Day, church services could publicly honor Sunday school teachers and helpers, children's workers, nursery attendants, prayer warriors—all those necessary, but unthanked people. Pastors could preach sermons about Barnabas, Lydia, Miriam, Dorcas, Martha, Ananias—wonderful, faithful servants of the Kingdom who are usually mentioned only in passing.

I suppose people could send the typical flowers and cards to former Sunday school teachers, pastors, and Christian friends, but what I think would really make Blessing Day special is to use blank cards and fill them in with your memory of the blessing that person gave you.

For example: To a Sunday school teacher—"Thank you for faithfully teaching my class during my eighth-grade year when I was so arrogant I thought I knew everything and only looked forward to Sundays because I enjoyed trying to turn you into a theological pretzel. You knew your Bible, though. I started studying mine just to match wits with you! You didn't tell me to shut up; you didn't lose your temper. You just continued to try to teach me about Jesus. Thank you for being instrumental in bringing me into the Kingdom. Thank you for being a blessing."

It may take me a while to get Blessing Day on the calendar, but in the meanwhile, is there someone who has been a blessing in your life? Has he been a "stretcher bearer" when you were wounded in one of life's many battles? Has she encouraged you? Has she spent time listening to your problems? Has he helped you grow in Christ? Drop each encourager a note and thank them. Share your joy in Christ with one who fostered it!

God keeps us so near to Himself that there will be little shining seeds scattered about. . .seeds that will bear a harvest of joy somewhere, sometime, and be melody to others in their heaviness. AMY CARMICHAEL

Serve the Lord with fear, and rejoice with trembling.

PSALM 2:11

For some, serving God is drudgery—like paying taxes. For others, it is considered a routine life-maintenance activity, such as cleaning the leaves out of the eaves spouts. But for those who truly love God, it is like a gift for a cherished one—a carefully selected, thoughtfully wrapped, joyfully given present of joy.

Do you serve the Lord with gladness? Let us show the people of the world, who think our religion to be slavery, that it is a delight and a joy! Let our gladness proclaim that we serve a good Master. CHARLES H. SPURGEON

Propagating Joy Through Worship

Church needs to be a joyful, accommodating place for little ones. Their very first memories of coming to God's house should be among their happiest. But in nearly every congregation are a few old cranks who feel children and their exuberant noises have no place in church services.

Fortunately, Jesus didn't feel that way. He scolded His disciples when they tried to prevent the children from "disturbing" Him. (But He threw a passel of misbehaving adults out of the temple!) A wise church will adjust to make worship meaningful and wonderful for kids, not only because they are the future of the church, but because Jesus said they point the way to joy for the rest of us.

The church we attended when our kids were little had done just that. All of us with small children and babies sat in an area reserved for us at the back of the church. The pastor had designated an under-the-balcony area for us, and we appreciated it. We wrestled with our kids, rocked them to sleep, fed them Cheerios and raisins, made hankie babies, played hangman and dot-to-dot—all things parents do to keep kids entertained in church services.

Unless they were seriously touched in the head, older folks really didn't want to sit back there with us anyway with all the distractions and confusion. They happily sat in front of the balcony overhang where they could actually see and hear without witnessing babies having a projectile vomiting contest.

One family in our church, the Bradys, invariably came in late. They traveled a distance to come, but I doubt it would have made any difference if they lived across the street from the church; they were just late people.

Since they were late by nature, and because even some people with babies really didn't want to sit back there with the rest of us, they sat up in the balcony with their two particularly lively little daughters, Vanna and Beatrice.

The little girls dangled songbooks off the balcony, dropped bulletins, used tissues, and toys all on the unsuspecting people sitting down below. The parents were seemingly unaware of the hazard created by their children, and blissfully observed the service in safety from their perch in the balcony while regular Sunday evening attendees avoided the area just under the balcony. Those pews became a sort of DMZ between parents with babies and folks who didn't smell of Eau d'Diaper Pail.

Until one evening. . .

Herman and Sarah Beeler were an elderly couple who had grown up on adjacent farms, then dated for thirty years before they decided they knew one another well enough to tie the knot. Childless after thirty years of marriage, they were tenderly romantic with one another and still held hands in church —a tribute to long courtship.

Herman and Sarah rarely came to church on Sunday evenings during the winter, as it got dark too early for them to feel safe on the roads. But as spring was turning into summer and the sap was rising in their ancient limbs, they decided to paint the town red and come to Sunday evening service. In an injudicious moment, they sat themselves under the balcony. Of course, the balcony was empty of Bradys just then, so they probably thought themselves safe.

Midway through the third verse of *Wonderful Grace of Jesus*, and unknown to Herman and Sarah, the Bradys moved into the balcony with their tiny bombers.

Soon the pastor was well into his sermon and the folks in the front were comfortably beginning to nod off. In the back, one by one, the babies were also starting to slumber. Parents were raptly and hungrily listening to the pastor as the only person they had heard speak all week who didn't begin every other sentence with, "He hit me first!"

In the midst of this calm, little Beatrice lofted a diaper of bird's-eye cotton off the balcony. It fluttered down through the holy air of the sanctuary, and in the back, three dozen pairs of horrified eyes beheld the diaper's parachuting decent from the balcony, watching in opened-mouth fascination to see where it might land.

Like an alighting dove, it landed gracefully over Sarah, squarely and completely covering her gray head. As her husband glanced over at her, a smile played across his lips. He reached up, gave the diaper a tug, and it fell from her head. In unison, their eyes locked upon each other as they—and the entire back of the church—convulsed in laughter. Meanwhile, the pastor was struggling with his own composure and train of thought.

While babies and youngsters are noisy, full of wiggles, and cause some spontaneous incidents, Jesus values them as part of His church. When they offer worship to God, it is spontaneous, joyous, and pure. It is this aspect that we staid adults should seek to emulate, knowing that God prefers their unpretentious praise to our regimented recitations.

As Jesus said, "Let the little children come to Me, and do not hinder them, for the kingdom of God belongs to such as these. I tell you the truth, anyone who will not receive the kingdom of God like a little child will never enter it" (Mark 10:14–15 NIV).

> *The spirit of happiness is sheer miracle. It is the gift of the happy God, as Paul names our heavenly Father in writing to Timothy. It is the gift of the God of love. He pours it out of His own fountains, through unseen channels, as He poured it upon Paul and Silas before their feet were taken out of the stocks and their stripes washed; for "no created power in hell, or out of hell, can mar the music of our Lord Jesus, nor spoil our song of joy."* AMY CARMICHAEL

Identifying Growing Joy

A voice tinged with amusement and aggravation startled me out of rapt concentration. "I should have known better than to ask a creative person to tie up boxes! I should have known you'd macramé them shut!"

I looked up to see my sister, hands on hips, regarding me with exasperation. With some guilt, I glanced at the several dozen boxes I'd already secured with string. Like a living diorama illustrating the evolution of knotting string around boxes, no two were tied exactly alike. Some had one handle created out of string; others had two. The box I held in my hands bore a ridiculous complication with three handles, one in the middle and one on either side.

This might not have been so bad if we weren't laboring under a time crunch. We had several hundred boxes to be tied and only about two hours to finish the task. Clearly, we had to hurry.

Damming up my creative juices, I tried to confine myself to a strict regimen of wrapping the string around twice lengthwise, around twice widthwise, and securing it with a square knot. Even using the exact same technique, though, we could tell at a glance who had tied which box. Little variations crept into my knots. It was just the nature of the beast. You could see my own unique personality being expressed even in something as simple as a knot.

So it is with people indwelt by the Holy Spirit. They are marked by His Presence. They bear the touches of His personality and power. People like this can look at a mundane task and find it a joyous deed to be done for Jesus. They can stare unflinching into the eye of adversity and rejoice that they are worthy to suffer for Christ. They see disaster as an opportunity for praise, because God is moving. They count it all joy when their faith is refined in the furnace of temptation, because they know they will emerge more fit for the Master's use. Their lives spread roots of joy to everyone who knows them.

All who would win joy
must share it.
Happiness was born a twin.

LORD BYRON

Take Time to Share the Joy

It's never too late to train your children to look for God's hand at work in their lives. Take a minute before the blessing at each meal and let every person around the table share something God has done in their lives that day. (Allow your dinner guests to pass if they don't feel comfortable sharing.)

This time becomes a witness to your family members and guests, and also helps make the blessing on the food more than just a formality. This is one way to propagate joy.

If we want joy to grow in our lives, if we want to spread it to everyone around us, then we must be careful to keep the soil of our hearts moist and soft, free from selfish weeds.

Life is one long joy,
because the will of God is
always being done in it,
and the glory of God
always being got from it.

F.W. Faber

Propagated from Seed

He was a sawed-off little squirt of a guy with bad eyes, hunched-back posture, and a very nasty attitude. When he was a kid, he was the presumptuous sort that the bigger guys waited on to beat the daylights out of after school because he'd humiliated them in class. He was academically bright—there was no doubt about that—but he had this self-righteous, know-it-all attitude that was downright irritating. Even as a grown man, he never hesitated to remind people that he had a blue-blooded family tree and that he had attended all the best schools. In short, he was the kind of person that people loved to hate.

Somewhere, somehow, he'd become a man with mission. He'd identified a cause that united the powers-that-be behind him, and he was tackling his objective with a coldly calculated passion. It was a distasteful job; it involved pushing around women and children as well as men, putting wailing families out of their homes, seizing their property, occasionally putting them to death. Not many other of the Pharisees, this group of religious elite, wanted to dirty their hands with that sort of task. All agreed it needed to be done, but most didn't have the aptitude or stomach for it like Saul did. Or the fervor. He was a one-man prosecution team. He sought out violators of the Mosaic Law, procured letters of indictment, arranged for false witnesses, stacked the jury, incited the crowds to violence, then held the coats of the executioners. It was a sweet little deal for the temple rulers; it got rid of the infidels while adding abandoned estates to the temple coffers, but it was still nasty business.

Saul enthusiastically went house to house, dragging families out into the daylight. Mom and Dad would stand there, stunned: the frightened children would be peeking out from the windows and doors. "Are you a believer in the Jesus Christ of Nazareth? Is He the Son of God?" he would demand. Then he'd step back, cross his arms, and watch them squirm, his weak little gimlet eyes flickering with malicious light.

Sometimes, the accused would deny they knew Him. Mostly, they would humbly admit they were His followers and be dragged away to prison, their children crying and clinging to their legs. A few, like Stephen, went down swinging, so to speak. He boldly faced his accusers, proved accurately from Moses and the Prophets that Jesus was the Messiah and so enraged the Sanhedrin that they had lynched him themselves.

Stephen was the first to die, and although others followed, it was Stephen's face and teaching that Saul could not erase from his memory. A still, small voice kept whispering, "Stephen knew the Truth; you are only fooling yourself. I will not die again," which only made Saul angrier.

A methodical man, Saul had pretty well decimated the Jerusalem church when he lifted his eyes to the strategically located Damascus. He gained permission from the Sanhedrin to establish a beachhead for his initiative through the Damascus synagogues. They gave him the legal authority and assigned a contingency of thuggish trained enforcers to accompany him. All prisoners would be extradited to Jerusalem for prosecution. It would be a glorious victory for Saul personally. Of course, God and His temple would profit, too.

With his mind fixed on his own glory, Saul's entourage set off north on the one hundred and seventy-mile journey to Damascus. The weeklong travel took him nearly the length of Israel and a little beyond, but oddly enough, it also took him near many places where Jesus had performed a healing, fed a crowd, delivered a demoniac, raised someone from the dead. If Saul could have avoided those places, he would have, because someone always managed to drop a little tidbit about Jesus the Christ, tell him a marvelous teaching spoken by the Man from Galilee, mention Him in some admiring way. Saul had to march directly through His home territory, where instead of mourning His death, they were still talking of His resurrection and ascension into heaven. Saul passionately wished he had letters from the Sanhedrin to arrest heretics in these towns, too. *In time,* he consoled himself, promising vengeance. *In time.*

But the stories and the teachings nagged at him.

It was late in the day when Saul and his companions descended Mount Hermon's rocky slopes and spotted the white, walled city of Damascus in the distance. A poet had called Damascus "the handful of pearls in a goblet of emeralds," and so it lay spread gloriously before them on the plain. Where the cool mountain breezes collided in the sky with the steamy air of the plain, a phalanx of thunderclouds boiled angrily, emitting bright bolts of lightning making the animals skittish and the men apprehensive.

Saul thoughtfully regarded the clouds. There was an old Jewish legend that clouds were actually angels hovering over the earth. If the clouds were white and scattered, the angels were simply listening for prayers.

But if the clouds were black, it was because judgment was about to be executed.

All along the trail, Saul thought of himself as bringing judgment upon the apostate. Now he wondered if judgment was instead about to fall upon him. In the clouds he saw the face of Stephen who had died bravely proclaiming that Jesus was the Son of God. He saw the gentle faces of men, women, and children who had steadfastly asserted the same even on pain of their deaths. Their courage couldn't help but give him pause; the prophecies about the Messiah, so beautifully fulfilled by Jesus, niggled in his mind.

"Oh, Yahweh! I want to know the truth about this Jesus," he prayed.

Suddenly, overhead, the clouds split as if cleaved with a

sword. A sheet of lightning pierced the air and hammered Saul flat on his face. The stroke didn't retract into the sky; it locked him to the earth as the skies spoke. "Saul! Oh, Saul!" the voice chided. "Why are you persecuting Me?"

Saul did not even attempt to look up. "Who are You, Lord?" his trembling voice spoke into the mud.

"I am Jesus, Whom you are persecuting. But get up! Go into the city! You will be told what to do!"

As the light retreated into heaven, large drops of rain began pelting to the earth. The temple soldiers rushed to Saul's side: They had heard the voice and the instructions. They wanted to quickly get him on his feet and into the city. They wanted to get away from Saul and Jesus. Dead or alive, Jesus was a dangerous Man.

Since Jesus taught His followers to pray for their enemies, someone must have obeyed. Someone must have begged the Holy Spirit to soften Saul's heart and to plant the Seed of Truth, and prayed that he would be forced see the Light. How their prayers were answered!

Saul opened his eyes. But the world was dark like his soul had once been, yet he had indeed seen the Light! While his physical eyes no longer saw, for the first time he could see Truth. This Light had taken root in his heart. Like so many other changed lives to follow, this miracle was wrought by Truth planted by the Spirit but watered and fed by the tears, prayers, and blood of the very ones whom he had sought to eradicate. Although within days, scales would fall off his physical eyes and partial sight would be restored, his mind was already seeing Light and Truth, and with Him, joy!

Common Destroyers of Joy

If you are a Christian believer who has no joy in your life, there is something very wrong because the Holy Spirit brings joy wherever He is. But like insects that decimate a healthy plant or thorns that choke out new growth, the encumbrances of life can rob you of God's joy. Prayerfully use this checklist—which is by no means exhaustive—to restore your life and heart to abundant joy.

- *Is there unconfessed sin in your life?* Check carefully. Has Satan deceived you into thinking that God doesn't know or care about the wrong things you do? I've got news: God both knows and cares, and your lack of joy is both symptomatic and a warning. In addition to preventing the Holy Spirit from filling your life with joy, unconfessed sin is like fish bait rotting in your heart. It makes life stink, poisons your present, destroys your future, and robs you of joy. Clean it out and experience the joy of restoration!

- *Are you ashamed of Christ?* Do your neighbors, friends, family, and coworkers know you belong to Him? Are you His alone—or when your Christians friends are not around, do you think of yourself as your own? Until you have surrendered your heart and life to Christ, so that you unswervingly identify with Him, you are not a healthy Christian. You can attend church, read the Bible, and "talk Jesus" with other Christians, but that only makes you religious. Look at it like this: It is as if you were married to one person and dating someone else. Neither relationship is likely to be joyous for long, and consequently, you won't be either. Unless you enjoy misery, you need to commit yourself completely to Jesus.

- *Have you said "no" to God?* Has God tapped you on the shoulder and told you to teach a Sunday school class, witness to your mother-in-law, start having devotions, or go to "Nineveh"? Here's a word of advice from Jonah, someone who told God "no": Beware of whales. Unless you relish taking up residency in a fish intestine, say "yes" to God, and you will find life exceedingly joyful.

- *Whom are you serving? You or God?* Some Christian believers consider God their Heavenly Errand Boy. They think they can order God around to do their bidding. These people are bound to be unhappy, because only God's paths lead to joy.

- *Are you going through adversity—and are you mad at God because you are in pain?* There are no easy explanations to trials and temptations; glib answers are simply hot air. However, know this: Jesus understands your pain. He is not a sadist. He will not let you suffer needlessly. With your cooperation, He will teach you something from your difficulties, and He will make something good come out of this pain. Jesus described a similar situation like this: "A woman giving birth to a child has pain because her time has come; but when her baby is born she forgets the anguish because of her joy that a child is born into the world. So with you: Now is your time of grief, but I will see you again and you will rejoice, and no one will take away your joy" (John 16:21–22, NIV). Hard as it is to believe, your pain will be temporary—but your joy in Christ will be permanent!

Create in me a pure heart, O God, and renew a steadfast spirit within me. Do not cast me from your presence or take your Holy Spirit from me. Restore to me the joy of your salvation and grant me a willing spirit, to sustain me. Psalm 51:10-12 NIV
(Written by King David after he was confronted with his adultery with Bathsheba and the murder of her husband.)

I am deeply part of the problem for which Christ died.

KEITH MILLER

The committed man of God is against sin, and all the powers of evil are against him. In such a warfare there is no intermission at all. The devil never takes five minutes' vacation! ALAN REDPATH

Look upon all sin as
that which crucified the Saviour,
and see that it is exceedingly sinful!

CHARLES SPURGEON

Identifying the Weeds that Destroy Joy
He Who Sees in Secret

"Whenever I have done wrong and then go back and make it right, I have joy," said Martha.

But when she does not, a host of problems beset her. "If I refuse to acknowledge the wrong and justify it, my life gets horrible."

Martha recalled a recent incident when she and her husband received an overpayment for their business. "It was one of the situations where we realized we could cash the check and no one—not the bank, the IRS, no one—would know. But God would," said Martha.

So they cashed the check anyway.

Almost immediately, Martha began to feel physically sick. "Every day I didn't feel good. I had such heaviness in my soul I couldn't even teach my Sunday school class."

The worst aspect of the situation was that in an effort to justify her own behavior, Martha began to find fault with everyone around her. "Do you remember the Scripture that says don't try to take the speck out of your neighbor's eye until you remove the log in your own [Matthew 7:1-6]? That's what I was doing. I was out of sorts with everybody. That money was eating at me!"

About then, the Lord hit her between the eyes with another powerful section of Scripture. "I was reading about laying up treasures in heaven, but the next verses grabbed me," said Martha.

This is the verse she read: "The eye is the lamp of the body. If your eyes are good, your whole body will be full of light. But if your eyes are bad, your whole body will be full of darkness. If then the light within you is darkness, how great is that darkness!" (Matthew 6:22–23 NIV).

Martha knew she and her husband had grieved the Holy Spirit by dishonestly keeping the money, and her guilt was making her sick and irritable. She determined to take the log out of her eye so she could again be filled with light.

"I told my husband, 'I'm going to put that money back.' As soon as I did, I felt better immediately.

"I've really learned that sin in my life saps the joy. I can't be happy with others when there's something wrong with me."

Nothing withdraws us from God but sin.
FRANCIS DE SALES

Sin is a tree with
a great many branches,
but it has only one root, namely,
the inordinate love of self.

KIRBY PAGE

Restoring the Joy: Clearing a Stony Heart

If it were easy to repair the wrongs we have committed, everybody would do so. Unfortunately, it's not. It takes courage and the grace of God.

Knowing the following facts will give you the impetus to make them right:

- *Sin—even when secretly committed—will enslave you.* Jesus said, "Whosoever committeth sin is the servant of sin." JOHN 8:34

- *The devil didn't make you commit the sin; you did it yourself.* "But every man is tempted, when he is drawn away of his own lust, and enticed."
JAMES 1:14

- *Sin keeps God from blessing your life.* "Your sins have withholden good things from you." JEREMIAH 5:25

- *If you sow sin, you'll reap sin.* "Be not deceived; God is not mocked: for whatsoever a man soweth, that shall he also reap." GALATIANS 6:7

- *God will forgive you if you ask.* "If we confess our sins, he is faithful and just and will forgive us our sins and purify us from all unrighteousness."
1 JOHN 1:9 NIV

- *You need to seek forgiveness of anyone you have wronged.* "Be ye kind one to another, tenderhearted, forgiving one another, even as God for Christ's sake hath forgiven you." EPHESIANS 4:32

- *If people wronged you, you must forgive them.* "But if ye do not forgive, neither will your Father which is in heaven forgive your trespasses." MARK 11:26

You Know You're Growing When You Can Apologize

Five Ways to Say "I'm Sorry"

1. Just do it. Go directly to the person, tell them honestly what you did without any excuses, and sincerely apologize. Say the words, "I'm sorry. Please forgive me." You might want to practice in front of a mirror first.

2. Send flowers or a small token gift accompanied by a card with a written apology.

3. Ask the person to lunch; after you order, before your food comes, tell them what you did and how sorry you are.

4. Sometimes you will offend someone and not be aware of it until later when the Lord pricks your heart. At those times, pick up the phone and call or talk to them face-to-face. Ask the question: "Did I offend you? If so, I'm sorry."

5. Occasionally, you will suspect that you have offended someone, but they'll say, "It's okay," and blow it off. You still need to apologize if the Lord is whispering that you have been offensive.

Whom have you wronged? Call them today and ask for forgiveness and experience joy!

> *It is obvious from faith in Holy Scripture that no one can sin without weakening or disturbing peace with God and in consequence with every creature.* JOHN WYCLIFF

We witness. . .by being a community of reconciliation, a forgiving community of the forgiven.

Desmond Tutu

Sin separates us from the joy God wants to give us. But when we are united with His Spirit, then we can hear His calling in our lives. The Holy Spirit will help us to grow in the direction He wants so that we can be effective vehicles of Christ's power and joy.

Growing in any area of the Christian life takes time, and the key is daily sitting at the feet of Jesus.

Cynthia Herald

I'm not all that I ought to be, but I thank God I'm not what I used to be. If I keep praying and asking God to make me to be what He wants me to be, some day I will be what I need to be. . . . In my walk with the Lord, I'm not saying I'm better than others—I'm just better than I was.

FRANCES KELLY

Listening to the Spirit's Calling in Our Lives

In March of Carrie's senior year in college, she felt pressured by everyone to decide what she was going to do with her future. The pressure had been building for a while, and Carrie knew that the time had come to receive more definite career direction from God.

It wasn't that Carrie didn't have a clue what she wanted to do—she did. She felt called to be a missionary.

"From the time I was seventeen and a new Christian, I felt called to be a missionary. But I didn't tell a whole lot of people because it wasn't a conventional job," said Carrie.

"There's not much spiritual heritage in my family. It was okay with my folks that I became a Christian, but they were looking at me cross-eyed because I went to Bible college. I knew if I said I wanted to go to the mission field, everyone would think I was loony.

"I knew my parents were scared to death that I was going to graduate from college with a degree I couldn't use. They thought I would sit at home the rest of my life."

Not only had Carrie spent four years gaining an education in preparation for the mission field, she had also broken up with her boyfriend because of it. "When we first started dating, he wanted to do mission work, too, but then he changed his mind," said Carrie. She was sad about the breakup, but she knew she had done the right thing in letting him go.

"I wanted to have the answers to the next step I should take. I didn't want to walk onto just any mission field; I wanted to know where God was leading," said Carrie. She admits she was almost in a panic over her future. She had no answers to everyone's questions about her future—including her own.

Almost paralyzed by her fear and indecision, Carrie began seeking the Lord. Then a speaker at her school encouraged her to start moving with the guidance God had already given her.

With that in mind, Carrie sent out E-mail to various missionaries and organizations, requesting information about their situation and what type of help was needed. "I really wanted to go to Nicaragua," Carrie said. "I saw a video on Nicaragua and God opened my eyes to that country. I could visualize myself there. I knew it was a country that had survived lots of turmoil.

I was intrigued that there were only four missionaries there when there were such pressing needs.

"I kept meeting people who had served in Nicaragua. Eventually, the Lord confirmed to me that the country needed people to work in discipleship and Bible teaching. That's what I wanted to do. It all made sense."

In response to her requests, several opportunities opened up, but they just didn't "fit" right for Carrie. Then one day as she was on the Internet, she saw an E-mail message for her with "Nicaragua" as the memo. Upon opening and reading it, she found this was exactly the opportunity she had been seeking. The missionary who wrote her had already checked things out with the Nicaraguan church leaders. They wanted her to come, too.

"I was so joyful at this confirmation of what God wanted me to do," said Carrie. "I wanted to tell someone, but I was the only one on the dorm hall. I had this wonderful news and nobody to tell!"

Carrie called a friend in California. This friend had been instrumental in leading Carrie to Christ, and she was among the first to hear of Carrie's call to the mission field. It was only natural that she should be the first to know Carrie's news.

"We screamed on the phone for a while," said Carrie. "Then I started running up and down the halls because I couldn't contain all the joy!"

In all thy ways acknowledge him, and he shall direct thy paths.

PROVERBS 3:6

And I will bring the blind by a way that they knew not; I will lead them in paths that they have not known: I will make the darkness light before them, and crooked things straight. These things will I do unto them, and not forsake them. ISAIAH 42:16

Steppingstones to Joy

Like Carrie in a preceding narration, we sometimes have a general sense of what God wants us to do, but we lack the specific details. That's okay. Don't feel you're lacking something essential just because you can see the eventual goal but can't discern even one step of the journey. Generally speaking, that's the way God leads—which is one reason why our relationship with Him is called a walk of faith.

Once in a great while, Hollywood correctly depicts a spiritual principle. In the movie *Indiana Jones and the Last Crusade*, the walk of faith is well illustrated. In order to find the Holy Grail, Indy must take a step of faith. He is standing at the mouth of a cavern that has led him to the edge of a great chasm, and he can see his goal: the door on the far side of a facing cliff. But beneath him yawns certain death.

Indy knows he is required to take a step of faith, so he takes a deep breath, closes his eyes, and steps into midair. But rather than falling screaming to the rocks below, he steps out on a cleverly constructed, yet totally camouflaged, stone gangplank that leads him to his goal.

Like Indiana Jones, you have to pursue your God-given goal by stepping out in faith, trusting Him to provide the support beneath your feet one step at a time. You can't always see even the next step—and sometimes it seems like you are stepping out into midair—but that's often the way God works to school us in faith and obedience. And this walk in the dark invariably leads to joy.

Joshua had a similar experience when leading the Israelites into the Promised Land (Joshua 3). He knew the goal: the land God gave them beyond the Jordan River. He had a vague idea of the path: across the Jordan River that was at flood stage. At God's command, the priests took the Ark of the

Covenant upon their shoulders and carried it down to the brink of the river. When they stepped into the water, the river stopped flowing and piled up in a heap so the Israelites could pass through. When they started toward the goal God gave them, He revealed the path.

And thine ears shall hear
a word behind thee, saying,
This is the way,
walk ye in it,
when ye turn to the right hand,
and when ye turn to the left.

ISAIAH 30:21

The steps of a good man are ordered by the LORD: and he delighteth in his way. PSALM 37:23

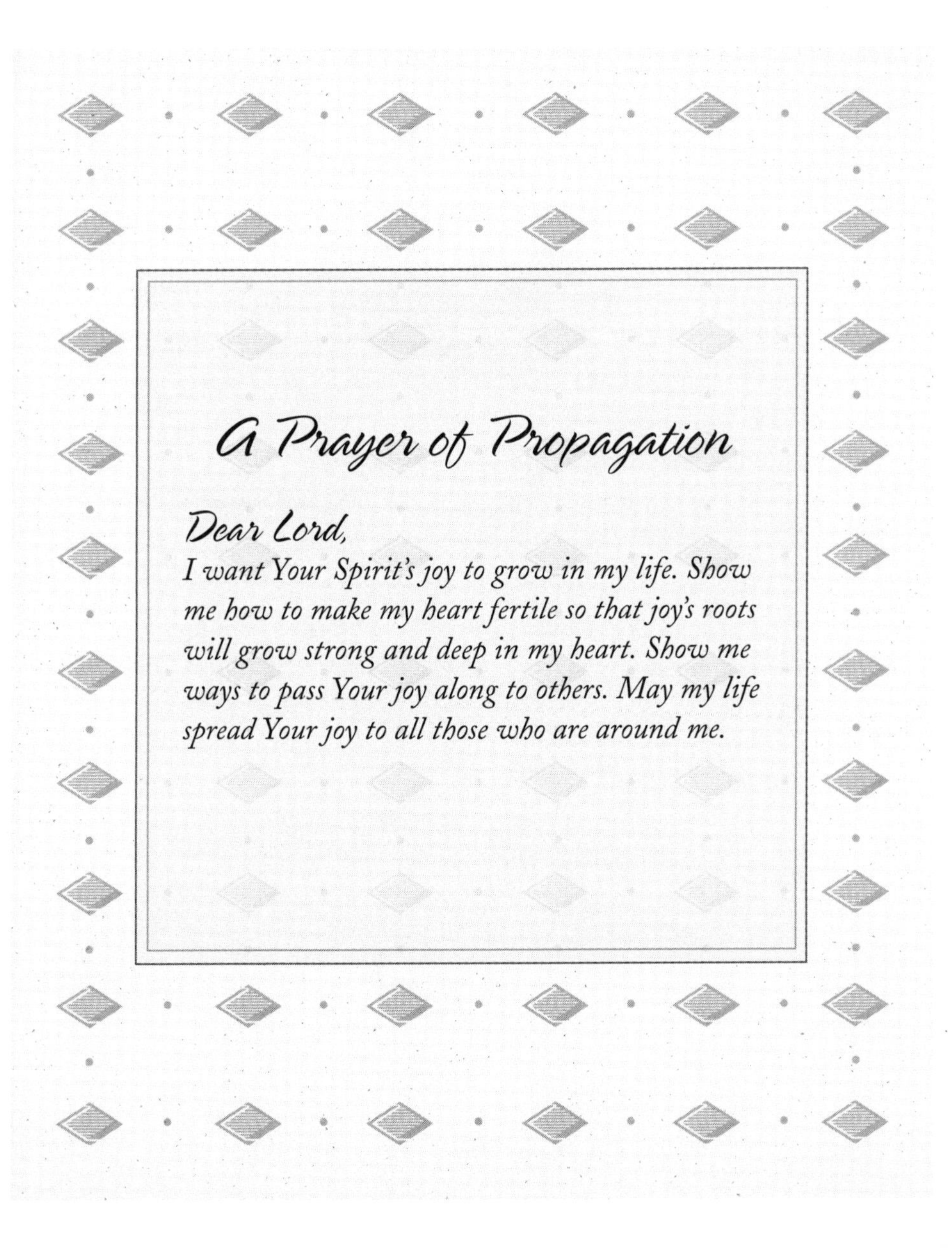

A Prayer of Propagation

Dear Lord,

I want Your Spirit's joy to grow in my life. Show me how to make my heart fertile so that joy's roots will grow strong and deep in my heart. Show me ways to pass Your joy along to others. May my life spread Your joy to all those who are around me.

Chapter 5

Commitment to God:
Joy's Blooming in the Garden of Gethsemane

They that sow in tears shall reap in joy. He that goeth forth and weepeth, bearing precious seed, shall doubtless come again with rejoicing, bringing his sheaves with him.
PSALM 126:5–6

Peace does not mean the end of all our striving,
Joy does not mean the drying of our tears.
Peace is the power that comes to souls arriving
Up to the light where God Himself appears.

G. A. STUDDERT-KENNEDY

When Christ prayed in the Garden of Gethsemane, we see the true blossom of joy that took root so long ago in the Garden of Eden. As He looked toward the cross, Christ sweat drops of blood—and yet His commitment to His Father—and to us—never wavered.

> *He. . .knelt down and prayed, "Father, if you are willing, take this cup from me; yet not my will, but yours be done." And being in anguish, he prayed more earnestly, and his sweat was like drops of blood falling to the ground.*
>
> LUKE 22:41–42, 44 NIV

Learn to Recognize the Joy of the Lord

HINT: IT APPEARS DURING ADVERSITY

> *Looking unto Jesus. . .who for the joy that was set before him endured the cross. . . .* HEBREWS 12:2

Divine joy appears in the wintry seasons of life when the cold blast of adversity hits us, at moments when everyone around us thinks we should be withering on the vine. It's a true oddity and a marvel, blossoming with an irresistible aroma like a tropical plant that spontaneously sprouts and thrives in Antarctica. It thrives and blooms whenever we are truly committed to God.

> *The discipline of dismay is an essential lesson which a disciple must learn. The danger is that we tend to look back on our times of obedience and on our past sacrifices to God in an effort to keep our enthusiasm for Him strong. But when darkness of dismay comes, endure until it is over, because out of it will come the ability to follow Jesus truly, which brings inexpressibly wonderful joy.*
>
> OSWALD CHAMBERS

A Joy That Endured

The Keys That Set the Prisoner Free

It wasn't fair, of course, or even legal. But because they released a poor slave girl from her demonic bondage, Paul and Silas were publicly stripped, severely flogged, and enchained. To add insult to their bleeding injuries, they were manacled to the walls of a subterranean jail cell in the company of

Philippi's most dangerous criminals.

This inner cell was a truly awful place. Sewage dripped from the ceiling and only the rats and vermin were healthy. It was like a crypt—except there the men were buried alive. When he left, the jailer took the torch with him, leaving Paul and Silas in utter darkness, still weak and bleeding from their beating.

Men quickly went insane in this environment. They muttered to themselves or moaned. So when the other prisoners first heard snatches of music from Paul and Silas, no doubt some of the saner ones thought these newcomers were already deranged. They listened to see what type of madness they would display. Would they shriek and beg? Laugh like maniacs? Cry?

To their amazement, they heard the sweet, ancient words from the psalmist set to melodies. They listened as the familiar words came from the cracked lips of these strange men. They heard prayers and praises offered to God. As the words echoed, a Presence washed the foul darkness with purity. Sorrows found solace, and loneliness was assuaged. How did this strange, unearthly joy come to fill this squalid place?

The joy of the Lord is your strength.

NEHEMIAH 8:10

What was the joy that Jesus had? Joy should not be confused with happiness. In fact, it is an insult to Jesus Christ to use the word happiness *in connection with Him. The joy of Jesus was His absolute self-surrender and self-sacrifice to His Father—the joy of doing that which the Father sent Him to do—". . .who for the joy that was set before Him endured the cross. . ."* (Hebrews 12:2). *"I delight to do Your will, O my God. . ."* (Psalm 40:8). *Jesus prayed that our joy might continue fulfilling itself until it becomes the same joy as His. Have I allowed Jesus Christ to introduce His joy to me?*

OSWALD CHAMBERS

Praise Demonstrates Our Commitment

Joy came to Paul and Silas because they did not assault the throne of God with charges of injustice, but rather with praises.

Joy came because although they didn't understand why, they understood Who. They knew God could overcome even the darkest evil with His goodness. They did not understand fully, but they were obedient, fully committed to the One they served.

Rarely is the curtain of God's purpose drawn aside in this life so we can see His plan. In Paul and Silas's case, however, we are given a glimpse to see what a marvel is God's power!

What happened was this: During Paul and Silas's praise, an earthquake shook the prison. Afterward, the cells were cracked open, shackles shaken free from the stone walls. The jailer assumed his prisoners had escaped, and he was on the verge of suicide when Paul stopped him.

The jailer was far more imprisoned, under far more condemnation, than were Paul and Silas when they were shackled to the fetid stones in the bowels of the jail. The jailer was spiritually handcuffed by the Father of Lies—but Paul offered him the key to his salvation: "Believe on the Lord Jesus Christ and you'll be saved. You'll be released. You'll be free. And like us, your soul will know joy even if your body is in prison."

This began a revival that rippled outward from the jailer to his family. From there it must have traveled still further. For all we know, it still ripples on today—all because God knew He could trust Paul and Silas to wisely use the keys of joy.

Consider it pure joy, my brothers, whenever you face trials of many kinds, because you know that the testing of your faith develops perseverance. Perseverance must finish its work so that you may be mature and complete, not lacking anything.

JAMES 1:2-4 NIV

The Flower of Obedience

A truly bumper crop of blossoming joy can be rare even among Christian believers. We must obey God to see joy's flower. And the best way for us to be truly committed to God is to praise, thank, and worship Him in times of trouble.

Most of us, though, would rather retreat into a corner of self-pity to whine and lick our wounds. We tend to blame God for our difficulties rather than thank Him for them. And again, we miss the opportunity to experience joy unspeakable, full of God's glory.

He that strives to draw himself from obedience, withdraws himself from grace.

THOMAS À KEMPIS

Joy in the Winter

Like many people in the throes of a time of testing, Mary felt utterly abandoned by God when one of her children died. The same year, she also had to bury three other family members, she had a miscarriage, her husband lost his job, they had a house fire, her best friend moved away, and her husband and remaining children had catastrophic illnesses—all within a six-month period!

"I felt like Job—complete with miserable comforters!" said Mary. "Believe it or not, people would say to me, 'You must have done something terrible for God to punish you like this!' I would rack my brain at night trying to think what awful sin I had committed, searching my heart for any unconfessed sin. I'm not perfect by any means, but God knew I was trying very hard to live for Him and rear my children right!"

Mary needed many years to work through the grief of that six-month period. Only then could she begin to distill life lessons from it.

"A beam of light didn't hit me and explain all the sorrows. I didn't get a devotional thought that made all the pain go away. I did, however, learn to ask God 'What?' instead of 'Why?' I learned to ask God *what* He wanted me to do with these lessons I was learning at such great cost; *what* He wanted me to do with all of the pain I was experiencing.

"I'm still asking God, 'What?' about many of the events of that six-month period (but I no longer ask, 'Why?')—and I'm amazed at how much He has taught me from the pain. Fifteen years later, I look back on those experiences as golden because they made me grow up as a Christian. They gave me deep understanding of the problems other people experience. I wouldn't have chosen to suffer all that, but God made Himself so real to me because of that time, and He gave me sympathy for others who are also in pain.

"I cannot say I have joy in the Lord today *because* of that time of trial—but I have learned to take joy from God's care for me even in the hardest times."

These things write we unto you, that your joy may be full.

1 JOHN 1:4

Of all of the beatitudes, the one that follows seems the most incomprehensible:

> *Oh, the God-given bliss of those who are persecuted because of righteousness, for theirs is the kingdom of heaven!*
>
> MATTHEW 5:10 (PARAPHRASED)

Why—and how—could anyone find persecution a joy? It is hard enough to be vilified when there is justification, but to be condemned, mocked, reviled, and falsely accused when one has done right seems an outrage rather than a cause for celebration.

Because this truth is so paradoxical to the natural mind, Jesus repeated it in the next two verses and added emphasis:

> *Blessed are you when people insult you, persecute you and falsely say all kinds of evil against you because of me. Rejoice and be glad, because great is your reward in heaven, for in the same way they persecuted the prophets who were before you.* MATTHEW 5:11–12 NIV

Imitation is said to be the sincerest form of flattery—but to imitate Christ in His sufferings and death is far more than flattery; it is our great honor. Martyrs experience God in a way that those of us who live lives of comfort and safety will never know. As God gave Christ grace to bear the cross, so He gives special grace to those who follow His footsteps through the Gethsemanes of life. Their reward is great in heaven. There they have everlasting joy!

> *We all go through pain and sorrow, but the presence of God, like a warm comforting blanket, can shield us and protect us, and allow the deep inner joy to surface, even in the most devastating circumstances.* BARBARA JOHNSON

The Garden of Gethsemane

An unmistakable air of anxiety hung over Jerusalem. Passover crowds always brought a certain tension as far-flung Jews crammed the streets and temple precincts, bringing strange customs and religious arguments in foreign tongues. The Romans added to the unease by beefing up their usual armed force lest the troublesome captive nation of Israel get any ideas about rebellion. But this year, the tension had an edge of significance. Something momentous was about to happen. Everyone knew it; even the spiritually insensitive Romans knew it.

Jesus knew what was happening. He was well aware of the half-truths about Him that were concocted and whispered behind the jeweled temple doors. He knew the rumors that swirled wildly through the impoverished streets and alleys. Plots and traps had been laid everywhere for Him, and He had known for some time that His life was about to publicly climax. He had sized up His twelve closest disciples, and he also knew which one would betray Him. When swords were drawn and lashes were administered, He was aware the rest would run like cockroaches before torchlight. The thought tore His heart, adding additional grief to His knowledge of what was before Him.

He had celebrated the Passover feast with His disciples, fully aware this was His last meal on earth in the company of

His dearest friends. As He watched them with a bleeding heart, they chattered like schoolboys through the symbolic courses, reciting from rote the Scriptures that told of Israel's deliverance from bondage. They argued politics a little among themselves, and they seemed genuinely aggrieved and shocked when He announced that one of them would betray Him. To a man, they vehemently denied it, but He knew better.

Now the meal was over. In the cool of the night, a thousand stars overhead, He led them to the lovely hillside garden a wealthy friend of His had put at His disposal. Just inside the stone wall, He let eight of the disciples find comfortable places to wait, while He took James, John, and Peter farther into the garden with Him to pray.

"My soul is overwhelmed with sorrow," He told them, "to the point of death. Stay here and keep watch with Me."

They didn't exactly understand His grief. To them, it appeared like the intense depression of a fatigued man, possibly because He had been doing so much teaching in the temple, so much healing—no wonder He was worn out! Or possibly, they reasoned, He was discouraged because the chief priests were openly opposing Him. *Overtired, overwrought, and overworked*, they thought as weariness and the heavy meal lulled them to drowsiness.

Alone in the quiet night, Jesus fell to the ground, His face to the sandy soil. The dew was settling and the fragrance of the night-blooming plants filled His nostrils. But grief and sorrow consumed Him. He groaned softly as tears flooded His eyes.

Both His life on earth and His purpose for coming paraded through His mind. He had left heaven at the bidding of His Father. He had taken on the body, the feelings, the passions, the pain of a man. Intent on fulfilling the Father's purpose, He had turned away from the tender, clinging glances of the young women. A wife was not in the plan. Nor was a family. Instead, He held in His arms the winsome children and babies of others.

For the last three years, He had preached, healed, consoled, prayed, and cried. The poor, the working class, the hungry, the sick, and the sinners loved Him, while the religious establishment hated Him, tried to trap Him, plotted against Him. And He loved them all regardless.

He thought next of the people He held especially close: His mother, sisters, and brothers; His disciples; Mary, Martha, and Lazarus; Salome, Mary Magdalene, and so many others. These He would leave behind, and He sorrowed for them, as any man would who would soon be bereft of all His family and friends.

"My Father," He begged, "if it is possible, may this cup be taken from me. Yet not as I will, but as You will."

He wanted to see His friends; He was desperate to see their dear faces once more. He stumbled back into the clearing where He left them. Even in the feeble light of the guttering oil lamp, He could plainly see they were asleep.

"Could you men not keep watch with Me only this once?" He cried, but their heavy breathing and soft snores were only slightly disturbed by the sound of His voice.

Peter smacked his lips softly and stirred slightly. "Master?" he muttered in his sleep.

"Peter!" Jesus cried. "Watch and pray so you will not fall into temptation! Your spirit is willing, but your body is weak!"

"Huh?" asked Peter.

Jesus repeated His words, but they echoed back in the night, mocking Him. Now He knew He was truly alone. No human friend could—or would—aid Him, and He could see the coming events with alarming clarity. The chief priests were plotting to kill Him. No doubt Judas would lead them to Him. When that happened, His disciples would abandon Him. After that, the chief priests would arrange to have Him tortured and put to death. He knew the prophecies concerning Himself:

- "False witnesses did rise up; they laid to my charge things that I knew not." (Psalm 35:11)

- "He was oppressed, and he was afflicted, yet he opened not his mouth." (Isaiah 53:7)

- "But he was wounded for our transgressions, he was bruised for our iniquities: the chastisement of our peace was upon him; and with his stripes we are healed." (Isaiah 53:5)

- "I gave my back to the smiters, and my cheeks to them that plucked off the hair: I hid not my face from shame and spitting." (Isaiah 50:6)

- "They pierced my hands and my feet." (Psalm 22:16)

Jesus knew all too well what lay ahead. He would be shamed, humiliated, tortured to death.

"My Father!" He cried, "if it is not possible for this cup to be taken away unless I drink it, may Your will be done!"

He waited, listening, searching the sky, hoping. He had seen men beaten; He had seen them crucified. He was all too intimate with that form of death and the torturous pain that accompanied it. His boyhood in Galilee was scarred by dark memories; Romans soldiers had routed out a large nest of local insurrectionists and crucified them, evenly spaced across the length of the Valley of Armageddon just over the hill from Nazareth. The dying cries of those men echoed in His ears day and night until the men finally died. Then the stench of their rotting bodies lasted for weeks. Just remembering made Him sweat.

He went back to His closest disciples. John was shivering in the cool air, so Jesus laid His cloak over him. He didn't need it just now anyway. As He stood looking at James and John, the sons of Zebedee, He recalled how their noisy relish for life had earned them the nickname "sons of thunder." His lips twitched as He thought of their famous contention that they should sit on His right and left hand when He came into His kingdom. He doubted they would still like that honor; He was about to come into His kingdom, and the chief priests would doubtlessly welcome having two of His closest followers to also nail to crosses!

Only their pride had made them ask for such positions of honor. They wanted to be esteemed as kings. They wanted to be like Jesus and be as powerful as God. Jesus choked; the bitter price of that pride would soon be foisted on His bleeding shoulders.

He stumbled back to His secluded spot and fell to the earth. Although He had been perspiring before, now the sweat poured freely off His face. *Sin. Separation from God.* He had avoided all His life anything that would come between Him and His Father, but now centuries of sin, eons of heartache, would be placed on Him. For the first time, He and God would be separated. The physical torture of the cross seemed a mere nuisance in comparison. He almost welcomed the cross as a diversion from the raw spiritual pain that would soon be dumped upon His conscience.

He wept freely. "My Father! If it is not possible for this cup to be taken away unless I drink it, may Your will be done!"

At that moment, a release came to His Spirit. Even there in that dark garden, despite all His sorrow, He knew joy again. After all, He was doing the will of the Father.

> *The "joy" that was set before Jesus was, we feel, knowing of the riches which would come to His brethren out of His death. In short, we are His joy, set before Him when on the cross. As we have seen, only as the circle of the love of Jesus becomes worldwide and as big as history will it be complete.*
> JOHN R. COGDELL

Although pride sowed the seeds of disobedience and sorrow in the Garden of Eden, the humility of Christ in the Garden of Gethsemane plucked them out and replaced them with obedience to God. This is joy in full flower!

Tribulation That Gave Birth to Joy
(Based on 1 Samuel 1, 2)

Men don't know how important bearing children can be to some women. The longing for children can be hardwired into the woman—like the love of chocolate.

Centuries ago, Elkanah didn't have a clue when he asked his childless wife Hannah, "Why are you weeping? Why are you downhearted? Don't I mean more to you than ten sons?" If she had answered that question honestly, he wouldn't have been a happy man, for the answer would certainly have been a resounding, "No!"

He didn't understand her longings for a sweet baby to care for and hold. He didn't know the actual physical pain of wanting a child so badly she was willing to plod the Valley of the Shadow of Death to give birth. And he didn't understand what it was like to be taunted because she couldn't have the children for which she longed so desperately.

Her childlessness had brought Hannah all the sorrow she could bear. She had slept alone when Elkanah took Peninnah as a second wife because she, Hannah, couldn't have children. She stood outside the tent, envious of the pain, when Peninnah panted in labor, and she wept with longing when each new baby uttered its first cry.

To add to her misery, no one gave her any sympathy for

her situation. Like a vulture sniffing out the dying, Peninnah sensed Hannah's secret sorrow and teased her relentlessly about her childless state. Mostly, it was little comments, small digs, constant sharp reminders—all calculated to show Hannah she was under God's judgment; her barrenness was proof. Hannah wasn't much of a woman, Peninnah said, because she hadn't birthed a child. Elkanah would one day realize she was an unproductive leech, Peninnah predicted, and put her away. And on and on and on. . . .

Celebrations were bitter because of the cruel teasing—and the longing. Elkanah would honor Hannah with double portions to demonstrate his love; Peninnah and her children would cleverly devise ways to make her life miserable. And in the end, Hannah would run crying from the feast table.

That was when Elkanah would offer his clumsy comfort: "Don't I mean more to you than ten sons?"

After one of these terrible episodes, in the depth of her sorrow, Hannah stood in the tent that served as the Lord's temple. She could see other families carefully training their children to love God and respect His commands. And she could see other parents—like the priest Eli—who permitted their children to be undisciplined hellions, racing in and out of the house of the Lord. Then there was Peninnah, so blessed with children, yet she used the Lord's feast days to school her children in attacking the defenseless.

In the anguish of Hannah's heart, she made a vow: *O Lord Almighty, if You will only look upon Your servant's misery and give me a son, then I will rear him to glorify You for the rest of his life!*

Only God needed to know her petition and promise. Only God needed to hear.

Nearly four years later, Hannah joyfully stood again in the temple. This time she held the hand of a young, three-year-old boy. The child was alert and well cared for. His quick dark eyes missed nothing.

"I asked God for this child," Hannah told the priest, "and He gave him to me. Now, I give him to the Lord for his entire life."

Then Hannah said a prayer of joyous praise: "My heart rejoices in the LORD; in the Lord my horn [or strength] is lifted high. My mouth boasts over my enemies, for I delight in Your deliverance.

"There is no one holy like the LORD; there is no one besides You; there is no Rock like our God." (1 Samuel 2:1–2 NIV)

When the sorrow passed and joy was born in her heart, Hannah kept the promise she made to God in her time of tribulation. Her promise was to glorify God. And she did.

Can God trust you to keep your promises? Can God trust you with blessing? Can He trust you with joy?

I tell you the truth, you will weep and mourn while the world rejoices. You will grieve, but your grief will turn to joy. A woman giving birth to a child has pain because her time has come; but when her baby is born she forgets the anguish because of her joy that a child is born into the world. So with you: Now is your time of grief, but I will see you again and you will rejoice, and no one will take away your joy. . . . Ask and you will receive, and your joy will be complete. . . . I have told you these things, so that in me you may have peace. In this world you will have trouble. But take heart! I have overcome the world.

JOHN 16:20–22, 24, 33 NIV
spoken by Jesus to His disciples

There will be moments in this life when a Christian has nothing but adversity and heartache while nonbelievers enjoy prestige and happiness. But remember: In the Spirit, moments of sorrow will turn to eternal joy.

Where to Find the Oasis of Joy in the Desert of Distress

Christians are often surprised when troubles come. For some curious reason, we think we should be exempt from them, despite the fact the Founder of our faith was Himself rejected by His nation, betrayed by one of His closest friends, abandoned by His inner circle, flogged, mocked, and crucified.

He did, in fact, flatly tell us that we would have trouble in this world. "In the world ye shall have tribulation," He told His disciples. Then He went on to say, "but be of good cheer; I have overcome the world" (John 16:33).

Tribulations will come—but Jesus has assured us He can ably handle them. All we have to do is: "Be of good cheer."

Praise is sometimes hard to muster in times of trouble because often the pain is all-consuming, especially when you have experienced a great tragedy. Yet know even in the darkest of times you are not alone. Jesus is with you even if He doesn't immediately heal your pain. You will learn from it, profit eternally, and reap joy.

There is a joy that springs spontaneously in the heart without any external or even rational cause. It is like an artesian fountain. It rejoices because it cannot help it. It is the glory of God; it is the heart of Christ; it is the joy divine of which He says, "These things have I spoken unto you, that my joy might remain in you, and that your joy might be full" (John 15:11). And your joy no man can take from you. Those who possess this fountain are not discouraged by surrounding circumstances. Rather, they are often surprised at the deep sweet, gladness that comes without apparent cause—a joy that frequently is strongest when everything in their condition and circumstances would tend to fill them with sorrow and depression.

It is the nightingale in the heart that sings at night because it is its nature to sing.

It is the glorified and incorruptible joy that belongs with heaven and anticipates already the everlasting song.

A. B. SIMPSON

An Example of Gethsemane Joy

Bales of Blessing

July 1986; Kewanee, Illinois

By the end of July, Rob could tell it was going to be yet another tough year for his farm. In fact, he didn't have to squint too hard at his horizons to see foreclosure and bankruptcy heading his way. The problem wasn't that he hadn't tried hard to make a go of his farm; he had. He possessed the know-how, the land, the muscle, the equipment, the drive—but the weather just wouldn't cooperate. Although the growing season was just beginning, he could smell drought and low farm prices in the air for the second year in a row.

His wife, Barbie, while trying to be supportive of her husband's plight and their impending financial disaster, felt her concentration needed to remain on the day-to-day housework and the care of the couple's three preschool children.

"I just had to go through the motions and do what had to be done for the kids every day," said Barbie. "And no matter how close we were as a couple, and although this was a crisis of survival, this was still something he just had to work through on his own."

Still, Barbie was overwhelmed by her husband's discouragement. "Rob was severely depressed," she said. "He was taking Prozac for his depression. Sometimes, I was afraid to leave him alone for fear he would take his life. There was one time that Rob was crying in one room and our son was crying in the other room, upset because his daddy was crying."

As he surveyed his neighbors losing their farms, Rob desperately tried everything to get out of his situation, but nothing yielded any results. He was too proud to ask God for help.

"I had put myself in this financial position by my own decisions," Rob confessed. "I didn't ask Him for help in making those decisions and I didn't want to ask God to help me now. I'd gotten into this by myself. I figured now I had to get myself out."

Then one July evening, Rob and Barbie did something totally uncharacteristic for early-to-bed, early-to-rise farmers: They stayed up long enough to watch a late-night television news program. The telecast featured an Iowa farmer who was taking relief aid in the form of hay bales to South Carolina farmers experiencing the most devastating drought in recorded history. The farmer's actions set Rob and Barbie to thinking of the few assets they owned.

They had several acres in a government "set-aside" program. Under this program, the government paid them to plant acreage in hay, then plow the crop under. However, because Illinois farmers had been financially struggling, the government released the hay back to the farmers. They could do anything they wanted with it—except sell it.

Rob and Barbie talked it over. They realized that the drought in South Carolina offered them an opportunity: They could give their good, prairie-grown alfalfa hay to a hurting South Carolina farmer, get a long-needed break from their own troubles, and teach their children something about giving, all at the same time. They decided to ask their pastor to contact a sister church in the hardest hit area of South Carolina to find a farmer who might need their hay.

Late July; Near Greenville, South Carolina

Ed and Lora Cable were milking 225 dairy cows twice a day, but they were inches away from being forced to sell their entire herd plus the beef and feeder cattle. They had poured thousands of dollars of seed and fertilizer into the ground. Their corn had sprouted, grew a foot tall, then was scorched to ash by drought as if a blowtorch had gone over the fields. The grass crops—hay and straw—barely germinated before the ground was baked to stone. Like many other South Carolina farmers, Ed and Lora had experienced several discouraging farm years, but this one was by far the worst that even the old-timers could remember.

The farm wasn't only Ed and Lora's, but it belonged to their children, too. Their three grade-school boys and their daughter took turns helping with the chores, choosing between the four-hour morning milking or the four-hour evening milking. In between, the calves had to be fed, pens cleaned, feed managed, and any number of other chores done. In good years, the whole family was needed to keep the farm running. Now it would require the grace of God.

Although Ed and Lora were Christian believers, an edge of bitterness was starting to creep into their hearts. While neighbors surrounding them were losing their farms to foreclosure, they had stayed on their faces before the Lord, asking for help. They were down to only a few days' food for the milk cows. There was simply no more hay to be bought and no more money to buy it. If the Lord didn't provide a miracle soon, they'd have to call the slaughterhouse to take all the animals. Bankruptcy would be certain.

Late July 1986; Kewanee, Illinois

Rob had looked everywhere for a job for himself off the farm, but no work was to be found. Now, feeling more like a failure than ever, he asked Barbie to go back to work. When they married, she had been a kindergarten teacher, but she had become a stay-at-home mom when their children were born. Perhaps, he suggested, she could find a teaching job again.

But the job market seemed to be experiencing a drought, too. Although Barbie applied for several teaching positions, school systems were hesitant to hire an experienced teacher whom they would have to pay more than a first-year teacher. In desperation, Barbie accepted a teaching job in the next county. It would mean a long drive away from her children, and the job was not what she wanted, but she took it. She would start in September.

Then the letter arrived from South Carolina. It told Rob and Barbie about Ed and Lora Cable, their farm, and their situation. In short order, Rob had his truck loaded, the kids and

Barbie on board, and life-giving bales of hay headed south to the Cables' farm.

They drove a couple of days to breach the gap between Illinois and South Carolina, but once they descended out of the cool highland mountains, they saw the abject devastation wrought by the lack of rain. The fields were dust, the lake beds were cracked and dried, the trees were dying. But the closer they got to the Cables' dairy farm, the broader the smiles and the more exuberant the waves of the people whom they passed on the highway.

"We weren't expecting anything," said Rob, "but we'd get the thumbs-up sign from people on the sidewalks. The whole town waved and honked at us."

When they pulled into the Cables' driveway, they discovered the Cables' entire church family had turned out to welcome them.

"This should put an end to the Civil War once and for all!" said the pastor, shaking hands with Rob and Barbie.

The hours that Rob and Barbie's family passed with the Cables were brightly tinged with joy, healing, and hope. The families immediately bonded from parent to child. They each understood the other's problems, and for the first time, everyone could share openly from the heart.

"It was like Lora and I were sisters and Rob and Ed were brothers," said Barbie. "Both guys were devastated by what was happening on their farms, and both felt like it was all their own fault." For Rob and Barbie, talking with the Cables eased their own pain and desperation; it provided a real sense of camaraderie, encouragement, and comfort.

While Rob and Barbie couldn't help the Cables financially, they could help them keep going until the weather broke and the economy improved. "We had feed going to waste and the equipment to get it to them. We had everything—but money," said Rob.

When their home church heard Rob and Barbie's report, they took up a special offering, providing fuel for four more loads of hay that tided over the Cables through Christmas. When the hay was gone from the Illinois fields, Rob found twelve acres of corn that could be had for nothing and hauled that to South Carolina, too.

Meanwhile, somehow, one day at a time, God provided for Rob and Barbie's needs. Grocery money would show up unexpectedly. Out of the blue, Barbie got another teaching offer, this one close to home. The price of land was such that Rob could sell off a few acres and a little equipment, and make a payment or two. The Cables assembled boxes of hand-me-down clothes to provide a wardrobe that stretched for several years for Rob and Barbie's kids.

But best of all, Rob's depression lifted so he could make good business decisions. With his pride broken, he made God his business partner on all further farm transactions.

"I learned to depend on God. Before, I was proud I was able to do everything on my own. This was the legacy my dad had built. But when I lost my pride and I got to the place where I didn't care what people thought, I finally reached the place where I knew I had to yield myself completely to God. Once I was following God, then God could work.

At last, Rob has learned how to tap into the joy that only comes from the Lord. "When you farm, you are at the mercy of God. Now, before I get in the field in the spring, I get on my knees and ask God to bless my efforts—and then I don't worry about it anymore. I don't have any control over what's going to happen, but God does. My depression is gone. Instead, my life is full of joy."

Be glad in the LORD,
and rejoice, ye righteous:
and shout for joy,
all ye that are upright in heart.

PSALM 32:11

The Shepherd answered Much-Afraid, "As long as you are willing to be called Acceptance-with-Joy. . . , you can never again become crippled and you will be able to go wherever I lead you!" HANNAH WHITALL SMITH

Let the heart of them rejoice that seek the LORD.

PSALM 105:3

The Best Way to Fight Discouragement

Anti-depressants have a huge market. Some may be necessary, but many pills taken for depression and anxiety could be avoided if a suffering person would only turn to the Great Physician.

Here's an entire medicine cabinet of joyous verses for the suffering soul. Take them all day long—no limit!—and call the Chief of Healing in the morning, noon, or night. Side effects include a closer walk with God, peace, and the growth of other spiritual fruit.

- *If you are discouraged with your job:* "Thou shalt rejoice before the LORD thy God in all that thou puttest thine hands unto." (Deuteronomy 12:18)

- *When you have enemies:* "My heart rejoiceth in the LORD, mine horn is exalted in the LORD: my mouth is enlarged over mine enemies; because I rejoice in thy salvation. (1 Samuel 2:1)

- *When you are alone:* "Glory and honour are in his presence; strength and gladness are in his place." (1 Chronicles 16:27)

- *When you need to discuss something sad or difficult:* "Till he fill thy mouth with laughing, and thy lips with rejoicing." (Job 8:21)

- *When grief is affecting your health:* "Your heart shall rejoice, and your bones shall flourish like an herb: and the hand of the Lord shall be known toward his servants. . . ." (Isaiah 66:14)

- *If someone you love has died:* "I will turn their mourning into joy, and will comfort them, and make them rejoice from their sorrow." (Jeremiah 31:13)

- *When you are working hard:* "Well done, thou good and faithful servant: thou hast been faithful over a few things, I will make thee ruler over many things: enter thou into the joy of thy lord." (Matthew 25:21)

- *When you need God's presence:* "Sing and rejoice, O daughter of Zion: for, lo, I come, and I will dwell in the midst of thee, saith the LORD." (Zechariah 2:10)

- *When you are persecuted for being a child of God:* "Blessed are ye, when men shall hate you, and when they shall separate you from their company, and shall reproach you, and cast out your name as evil, for the Son of man's sake. Rejoice ye in that day, and leap for joy: for, behold, your reward is great in heaven: for in the like manner did their fathers unto the prophets." (Luke 6:22–23)

- *When you have needs:* "Hitherto have ye asked nothing in my name: ask, and ye shall receive, that your joy may be full." (John 16:24)

- *When you have adversity:* "In the world ye shall have tribulation: but be of good cheer; I have overcome the world." (John 16:33)

- *When you are distressed or ill:* "I take pleasure in infirmities, in reproaches, in necessities, in persecutions, in distresses for Christ's sake: for when I am weak, then am I strong." (2 Corinthians 12:10)

- *When you are being tempted:* "My brethren, count it all joy when ye fall into divers temptations; Knowing this, that the trying of your faith worketh patience. (James 1:2–3)

The hope of the righteous shall be gladness.

PROVERBS 10:28

Growing Morning Glories

Are you ever afraid of the dark? Of what's lurking out there, hidden beneath a cloak of night, waiting to grab you? Not since you were about six, you say. Okay, but have you ever tossed and turned the night away worrying about what the next day, the next week, or the next year will bring?

When worry robs you of your sleep and peace of mind, here are some suggestions to bring back the joy of the Lord:

- *Open your eyes*—If you could see into the spirit world, you likely would see angels of God and demons of Satan fighting over your peace of mind. But what you definitely would see is Jesus. Wherever you are, wherever you go, no matter how deep the trouble, He is beside you. He promised to "never leave you or forsake you" and to be with you "even unto the end of the world." Acknowledge His presence and bask in it. Pour out your heart to Jesus who understands; He is able to do exceedingly more than you ask or think. Jesus had His own Gethsemane and remained faithful. He'll get you through yours.

- *Count your blessings*—Some people count sheep; try counting blessings instead. Find a blessing in your life for every letter in the alphabet and thank God for each.

- *Get on your knees*—Don't just lie in bed tossing and turning! Climb out of the sack and start praising God. (For those who are confused about the difference between thanksgiving and praising, thanksgiving is thanking God for *what* He has done while praising is thanking God for *who* He is.) Expect to find yourself getting suddenly sleepy. Satan hates it when we praise God. He'll sing you a lullaby himself just to keep you from praising.

- *Raise your hands*—If someone pointed a loaded gun at you, you would indicate surrender by holding up your hands. When you hold up your hands before the Lord you are surrendering your problems to Him. Release your problem to God. He'll take it out of your feeble hands and carry it in His nail-scarred almighty ones.

Remember—All problems are temporary, including the ones keeping you awake, so remember: *Weeping may endure for a night, but joy cometh in the morning* (Psalm 30:5). Start now to thank God for His answer to your need.

I have learned the condition
to having constant joy.
The condition is allowing
Jesus to sit at the
control center of my life.

MARABEL MORGAN

Finding Joy in the Darkness

In the nighttimes of your life when problems come, when you say in your heart, "I submit to this and I know God will bring good from it somehow," you'll discover that God gives grace to the humble. He lifts up those who submit to Him.

Joy That Blooms in Grief

Every day is tough for someone working through the loss of a loved one. Only those who have walked through the Valley of the Shadow of Death can know the emotional, and yes, physical pain of those who are mourning. Counselors say it takes up to three years to recover from the loss of someone who is significant in your life, but those who have suffered a great loss can tell you it takes a lifetime to reconcile the grief to the soul.

Birthdays, holidays, and death anniversaries are usually the worst days to live through. . .but there is a way to bring the joy of the Lord to a day of loss and thus redeem the pain: Consider "adopting." It will help ease the pain of your loss, bless someone else, and you will find it is more blessed—or joyful—to give than receive.

Choose someone who is roughly the same age and gender of your lost loved one and cook up a way to bless them on those tough days. Ask the Lord to send someone to you. Check with your pastor for suggestions of someone who needs the type of blessing you can provide. People like social workers, nursing home administrators, and scout leaders can also tell you of individuals who can use a little of the love your heart holds for your lost one.

If you have lost a young child, consider giving a toy, clothing, a video, books, or an afternoon's activity, such as a trip to a museum to a child in need.

If you have lost a teenager, consider giving money or tickets to a Christian concert. Books, CDs, and videos are also good. Perhaps, if it isn't too traumatic for you, you may volunteer to be a youth sponsor in your church.

If you have lost an adult child, look for a college-aged student who can use your encouragement, care packages, and some occasional money. Or perhaps you will find a young family who can use a surrogate grandparent.

If you have lost a parent, borrow a mother or a father by inviting someone to dinner at a nice restaurant or in your own home.

If you have lost a mate, your job is a little harder, because some people might misconstrue your intentions. However, lots of other people have lost mates, too. Consider forming a cozy group of people to go to movies, plays, dinner theaters, craft fairs, cruises, church activities, and all the other things you would enjoy doing with your mate.

One Christian divorcée who loved to cook found companionship, healing, and a great way to witness by inviting a group of divorced people to share in a Valentine's Hawaiian luau at her home. Each person chipped in a few bucks, she bought the food, and then everyone helped make the meal, ate, and cleaned up. They played games, laughed, and talked. Toward the end of the evening, she shared a short devotional.

She planned a theme dinner as a once-a-month event, and over time, several of her new friends found the Lord. (Not surprisingly, some found new mates, too.)

Beholding His Face with Joy

"Are you asking one another
what I meant when I said,
'In a little while you will see me no more,
and then after a little while
you will see me'?
I tell you the truth, you will weep and mourn
while the world rejoices.
You will grieve,
but your grief will turn to joy."
the words of Jesus in

JOHN 16:19–20 NIV

For a Christian,
the sorrows in this life are
like labor pains of joy.

The Joy of His Presence

When Loraine's husband walked out after thirty-eight years of marriage, she was shocked, but the greatest havoc in her life was yet to be wrought.

"It wasn't losing my husband that was the biggest loss," said Loraine, "because the marriage had been dead for years. It was losing my entire life. It was going from having a full life to being completely, totally alone."

Loraine described how she had spent the decade since her children had flown the nest caring for either her own elderly parents or her husband's. About the same time her husband left, she was forced to admit her father to a nursing home.

"I went from having a husband and a father to care for, laundry to do, meals to cook, all kinds of responsibilities—to absolute silence. The phone stopped ringing, nobody came, no one was in my big house but me."

In the silence, Loraine hit bottom. She sometimes wept for days at a time. At the same time, though, she poured out her heart in prayer and studied her Bible for answers to her dilemma.

"For many years, I had been too busy for God, but when my world stopped, He was all I had left. I had known the Lord nearly all of my life, but in my grief and repentance, I found Him in a way that is sweet beyond description!"

Loraine describes experiencing the presence of God in a way she says she never knew she could. "It sounds strange, but God has been so near to me in this time of sorrow that I almost dread leaving this place of grief. I want to continue to experience His presence like this. I can't even describe it, but I've felt total joy through this terrible time, because I've been so aware of Jesus. The greater the grief, the sweeter He is."

Loraine knows her life will continue to change. After being out of the workforce for many years, she has found a unique job to support herself. "While I would never want to go through something like this again," she admits, "I still will never fear heartache again, because I know even in the deepest sorrow, the presence of the Lord gives joy!"

The path of trouble is the way home. Lord, make this thought a pillow for many a weary head!

CHARLES H. SPURGEON

If thou can be still and suffer awhile thou shalt without doubt see the help of God come in thy need.

THOMAS À KEMPIS

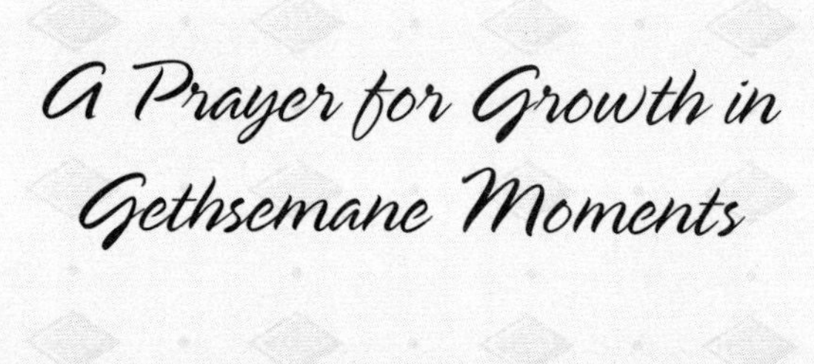

A Prayer for Growth in Gethsemane Moments

Oh, Lord, my heart is broken. But You have promised that You will give beauty for ashes, the oil of joy for mourning, and the garment of praise for the spirit of heaviness (Isaiah 61:3).

You will replace my confusion so that I will rejoice in the life You have given me. You

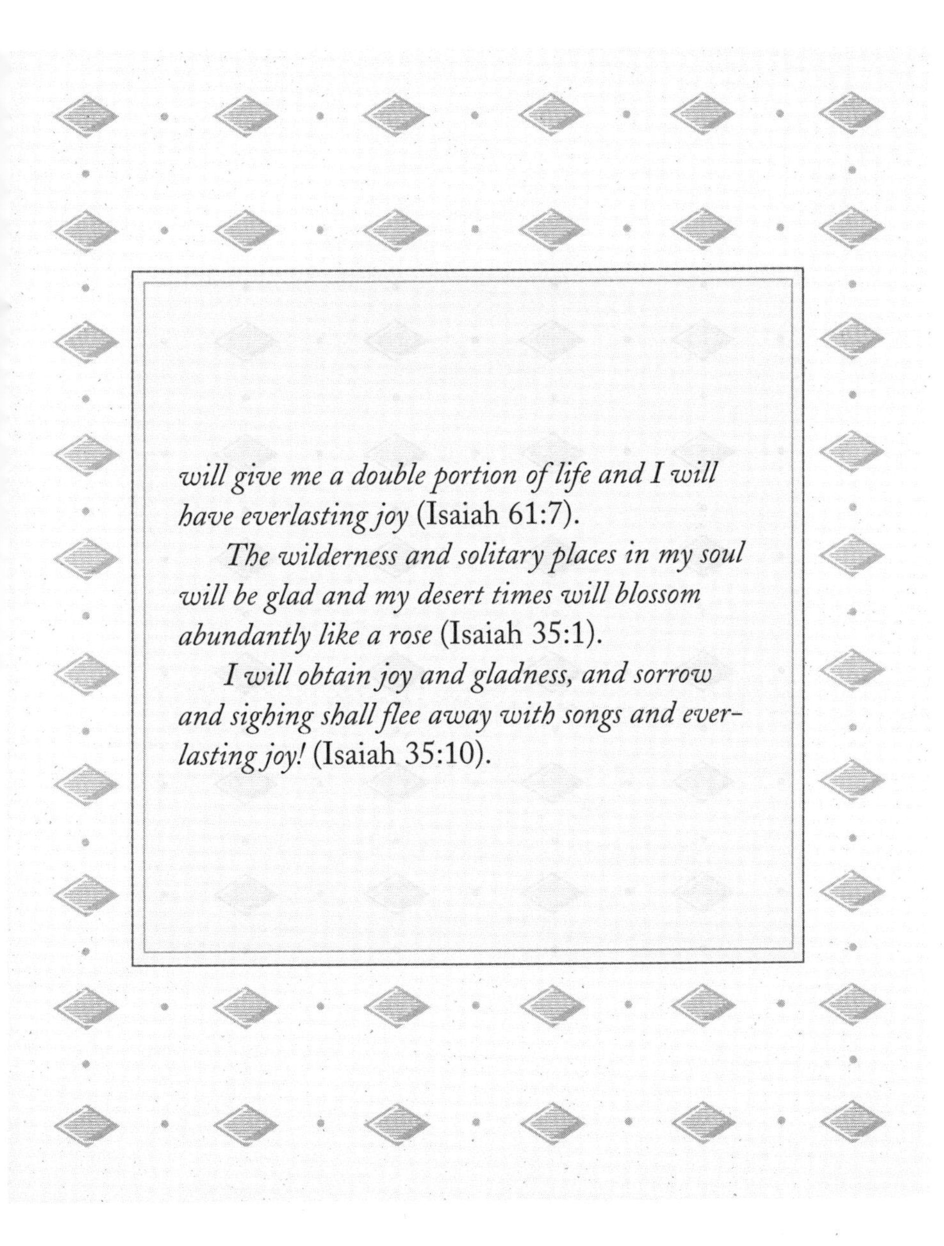

will give me a double portion of life and I will have everlasting joy (Isaiah 61:7).

The wilderness and solitary places in my soul will be glad and my desert times will blossom abundantly like a rose (Isaiah 35:1).

I will obtain joy and gladness, and sorrow and sighing shall flee away with songs and everlasting joy! (Isaiah 35:10).

Chapter 6

Joy's Fruition in the Garden Tomb

These things have I spoken unto you,
that my joy might remain in you,
and that your joy might be full.

JOHN 15:11

Any woman who is filled with joy, His joy, can also tell her Heavenly Father, "I like whatever state I'm in right now the best." And not just tell Him—but shout for joy!

MARABEL MORGAN

The roots of our joy reach back to the foundation of the world; they are sustained by the Holy Spirit alive in our hearts; by His power, they grew strong, and in life's Gardens of Gethsemane they bloom; now, in that garden tomb where they laid Christ's lifeless body, they burst in glorious resurrection fruit.

The Victory Garden of Joy

The Seeds of Eternal Joy for All Humanity

She awoke before dawn from a fitful, disturbed sleep and lay quietly listening to the soft snores and steady breathing of those in the household. Although she was exhausted, a heavy responsibility lay upon her shoulders, one which she both loathed yet felt honored to fulfill. Today, with Passover and the Sabbath over, she and the other Mary would go to the tomb and anoint the body of their Lord. No one else could do it. Everyone had their reasons, but Mary didn't understand how they could stay away from His tomb. It was the only place she wanted to be.

How can they claim to love Him in life, but abandon Him in death? puzzled Mary Magdalene. *Where are the disciples who were going to be so powerful when He came into His kingdom? Hiding? Certainly not here to prepare His body for burial!*

The last few days had been terrible, and she had only been able to sleep for a few stolen moments since the crucifixion. Every time she drowsed off, the slightest noise made her relive one of the many horrors—the fist pounding on the door announcing His arrest; the whistling of the leather whip and His moans of pain from the flogging; the sickening ring of steel-against-steel when they nailed through His hands and feet into the planks; His heart-rending cry, "My God! Why do You forsake Me?"; and finally, the whispered, "It is finished!" These memories brought her clawing her way out of the replayed nightmare—only to discover afresh that the nightmare was true.

Then there were the earthquakes—another one just an hour earlier—storms, damage to the veil at the temple, weird reports of appearances of people long dead, rumors, and fears. Those things would have been awful by themselves, but the centerpiece of her grief remained the death of the Master.

Mary, His mother, frail to begin with, was now prostrate with grief. She was questioning His birth, His life, and certainly His death. What had gone wrong? What had happened to God's plan? Surely this was not it!

The disciples hid in fear of their lives. Who knew the lengths to which the Jewish rulers would go to stamp out every memory of Jesus' teaching and His miracles. Perhaps every reliable witness would have to die. *And that would include me*, Mary Magdalene thought, but she did not care, for her reason for living was lying dead and stiff in the tomb of Joseph of Arimathaea.

She thought back to her first face-to-face meeting with Jesus. It had been in those bad old days when she supported herself through selling her body, and she had looked at every crowd as an opportunity for commerce. As she worked the edges of the mob surrounding Jesus, she couldn't help but overhear His sermon and see His miracles. His words traveled over the crowd's clamor and gripped her heart. She had plugged her ears and screamed out loud with the pain of her sin—until Jesus put His hand on her shoulder and ordered the inhabiting demons to leave. They did not wish to go quietly, but He ordered them to hold their peace and come out.

Their exit left her weak—and without an occupation. Dear Mary, the mother of Joses and Salome, took her in, and now she was counted among their kinfolk. Now her friend had agreed to accompany her to the grave and care for the body.

Mary Magdalene quietly unwrapped herself from her cloak and stood. In the darkness, she found the other Mary and shook her awake. They silently picked up their baskets and jars prepared the night before and slipped out into the gloom of false dawn. Covering their faces, they hurried through the maze of streets toward the gates of the city.

The iron hinges moaned when the keeper swung them open to let the two women pass through the city walls. The grinding noise and the grunts of exertion from the burly keeper reminded Mary they would face the stone at the mouth of the tomb when they reached their destination. How would they move it? Could the soldiers be convinced to help? Would the gardener?

Nothing to do but try, thought Mary. *And even if I can't get in the tomb, at least I can be near the One who changed my life.*

Dampness clung to the women's hems as they climbed the rocky path through the graves and out to the garden. Then, as they reached the garden gate, the ground shook violently again and the valley of the dead seemed to let out a moan as the earth heaved and buckled. An involuntary scream escaped Mary's lips, and the women clung to one another for support. After a few seconds, the earth again stood quiet. Trembling, the women entered the garden.

Before their eyes, they could see what they hoped—but feared. The tomb gaped open, obviously empty, the stone flung down the hillside. Roman soldiers lay scattered on the ground like the casualties of a mighty battle.

Upon the rock sat a huge man with flashes of light dripping off him. He seemed to be watching them, waiting for them to approach. When they drew near enough, he said, "Don't be afraid! I know that you are looking for Jesus, who was crucified. He's not here! He's risen from the dead! Remember: He told you He would."

The women stared at him in disbelief.

"Come here and look at the place where He was laid," the man invited. Mary got the distinct feeling the man was almost laughing at them for not instantly believing his words.

Hesitantly, the women approached the tomb and peeked inside. The rolls of linen they had so tearfully wrapped around His still form now lay in tidy loops as if He had passed through them, leaving them empty. The napkin covering His head was neatly folded and laid to one side.

The bright man spoke again, his voice warm and friendly but filled with authority. "Go tell the disciples He has risen! They will see Him! Go now! I've told you what to do."

Mary hesitated. The man was impressive, but he was not the Person she wanted to see. She longed for the sweetness of Jesus' presence, the joy, peace, and acceptance she felt when He was near.

Little did she know the events in this Garden paved the way for the coming of the Holy Spirit. The Resurrection meant she would never be without Jesus—or His Joy—again!

The whole history of the Christian life is a series of resurrections. . . . Every time a man finds his heart troubled, that he is not rejoicing in God, a resurrection must follow; a resurrection out of the night of troubled thought into the gladness of the truth. GEORGE MACDONALD

She had survived some of the meanest blows life can deal a woman—abuse, poverty, divorce, homelessness—but she had never wavered in her commitment to her Lord. When she knew breast and liver cancer was going to literally eat her alive, she handled it like she had so many of life's other nasty little incidentals—she looked it in the eye and dared it to try to take her soul, her joy, or any other fruit bequeathed to her by the Holy Spirit. Her attitude was: "My soul belongs to Jesus! See Him, Mr. Cancer, if you're planning to mess with me!"

Since she was tough, tenacious—and also perhaps because she was a little eccentric—the cancer took a while to complete its work. In the process, however, it robbed her of her job, her independence, her hair, and a goodly amount of her dignity. When she finally died, she looked better in the coffin than she had for weeks before.

But the mood around her bier was one of celebration, not only because she was released from a life of pain, but also because she had begun a life with no pain forever and ever with her Beloved. She was in Eternal Joy.

If there is not joy in religion, you have got a leak in your religion.

BILLY SUNDAY

Resurrection Joy

You couldn't help but like Davie Kruger, but there was no denying he was the town drunk. He made a good wage but almost single-handedly supported the local tavern with his purchases. When he was drinking, he was benign and humorous and fun-loving—the life of the party. When he was sober, he was much the same except that he was less inclined to suddenly burst forth with the chorus of *Red Wing*, and he was perennially worried about his finances. Every weekend, he drank up his paycheck before he could pay the bills.

His wife and little daughters loved him dearly, but they also worried. Finances—or lack thereof—were a big concern for them, but the state of Davie's health was even more frightening.

He had been drinking heavily for a long time, and the alcohol had taken its toll.

Careworn Mrs. Kruger and the girls attended a tiny, wooden-framed, ancient country church besieged on the north by an army of tombstones. Lying among them were most of Davie's relatives, pre-embalmed and helped into early graves by Jim Beam and Jack Daniels. If something didn't happen soon, Davie would soon be joining his kin.

For years during Wednesday evening prayer meeting, Mrs. Kruger had been begging God to make her husband attend church, get right with Him, and be delivered from alcoholism, but Davie always told her, "Aw, honey, if I ever went to the altar, the church floor would collapse!" Once in a while on Sunday morning, though, she'd get him stuffed into his good suit, and he would attend services, looking miserable, hungover, and pained at the singing and sudden noises. His appearances were rare, so the floor seemed safe.

Then the little church planned a revival service, and the community was abuzz. A woman evangelist was coming—a novelty—and her husband was supposed to be a wonderful musician. Davie had been drinking more heavily than usual and was in very bad shape, so Mrs. Kruger called everyone she knew to ask them to pray that Davie would come to the revival and get saved before it was too late. They must have prayed—or the lure of a woman evangelist and good music was very great. Anyway, a stone-sober Davie attended every night of the two-week revival service.

On the last night of the service, the old church was packed to capacity with a standing-room-only crowd. The altar was full of penitent sinners and people praying with them. Mrs. Kruger and the girls were there, praying for Davie. Davie was back in his seat, clutching the pew ahead of him, his knuckles white. Suddenly, he jumped up and bolted for the back door. With his hand on the doorknob, he froze, wheeled around, and ran to the altar. The moment his knees touched the polished boards, the entire church floor dropped six inches. Davie didn't even notice: He was attaching himself to the True Vine and drinking the new wine of the Holy Spirit.

After revivals, some of the new converts generally thin themselves out by gradually forgetting their commitment to the Lord. People watched Davie as a prime candidate for this, but he didn't. His conversion changed the entire landscape of the town.

Davie's favorite watering hole closed for business, sat empty a while, and much later, became a secondhand junk shop. The little church built a new building on the edge of town. Here Davie and his missus saw their new baby son dedicated to the Lord. They eventually witnessed the marriages of all their children except one daughter, who became a missionary in Haiti and got married down there.

Years later Davie joined the rest of his family in the old churchyard; but until that day, he joyfully loved to tell people, "I am an alcoholic saved by grace. I always said that the floor of the church would fall in if I ever got saved. I must be saved, because when I asked Jesus in my heart, the floor dropped six inches!" Not everybody gets such an obvious physical manifestation to verify salvation, but all receive the same confirmation: the joy of the Lord. Unlike the euphoria that alcohol offers, the Spirit's joy lasts beyond death and into eternity.

> *Joy is not created by possessions, or by positions, but a Person—Him! Let me add, however, that joy is not an inflexible, unvariable thing. It is not a deposit placed in the soul after salvation without any chance of deterioration. . . . Joy requires at least two conditions: submission and service.* LEONARD RAVENHILL

A believer's greatest joy is not what he has done for Christ, but what Christ has done for him. There are those who mourn for the natural losses in this life, the loss of a child, a mate, a parent, a career, or their health—the list is endless because this life is characterized by loss. But that's why the comfort of Christ is so inexpressibly sweet!

Unlike any other, He understands the wrenching, bleeding hole left in the heart by these losses. He was the one who said,

"Let not your heart be troubled, neither be afraid," when He spoke of physical death and new life to come. He was the one who wept at the tomb of Lazarus, even though He knew all about heaven. Although He knew He could—and would—raise Lazarus from the dead, tears still came for the loneliness of His loss.

But Jesus restores! He is the Master Comforter! His comfort is as varied as the souls that are hurting. For some, He gives them a shot of "spiritual anesthetic" to help them through their sorrow. For others, His presence is very near and sweet. Over time, His comfort is healing and transforming. When Jesus comforts, there is joy. Resurrection joy!

> *The things we try to avoid and fight against—tribulation, suffering, and persecution—are the very things that produce abundant joy in us. "We are more than conquerors through Him" "in all these things"; not in spite of them, but in the midst of them. A saint doesn't know the joy of the Lord in spite of tribulation, but because of it. Paul said, "I am exceedingly joyful in all our tribulation" (2 Corinthians 7:4).* OSWALD CHAMBERS

The word of the Lord spread through the whole region. But the Jews. . .stirred up persecution against Paul and Barnabas, and expelled them from their region. So they shook the dust from their feet in protest against them and went to Iconium. And the disciples were filled with joy and with the Holy Spirit. ACTS 13:49–52 NIV

When Paul and Barnabas sowed the seeds of Christian joy, rumor and jealousy caused good people to turn into pillagers of the faith. The plain fact was the Jews were infuriated that the privileges they possessed as God's own special people might be extended to the Gentiles. As it has been said, "The Jews saw the heathen as chaff to be burned; Jesus saw them as a harvest to be reaped for God."

You can't know Resurrection joy unless you've first experienced the cross. Holy joy is a unique emotion known only to those who have gone through the crucifixion with Christ. Once you have, then fear is weeded out of your life. Courage planted by the Holy Spirit springs up with supernatural speed and vigor. Discouragement wilts and new counsel from the Holy Spirit is discovered with clarity and joy. Your life is laden with the Spirit's sweet fruit.

And ye became followers of us,
and of the Lord. . .
with joy of the Holy Ghost.

1 THESSALONIANS 1:6

Bearing Fruit

Finding God's Steppingstones

There's a corny old joke about two clergymen and a rabbi who were fishing from a boat. As the day passed, the clergymen and the rabbi began to discuss the merits of righteousness by faith in Christ versus the Jewish belief that righteousness comes from keeping the Law. No matter how long they talked, the rabbi remained unconvinced.

As the day wore on, one of the clergymen realized he had left his bait bucket on the shore, so he stood up, walked across the water, fetched the bait, casually strolled back across the water, and climbed into the boat. The rabbi was astonished, but he swallowed hard and said nothing. A little later as lunchtime approached, the second clergyman stood to his feet, walked across the water, got the picnic basket, walked back across the water, and got into the boat. Again, the rabbi only silently stared, but the two clergymen could see he was fighting a mighty internal struggle.

Finally, the rabbi stood to his feet and announced he was going to fetch something on the shore. Before they could stop him, he stepped out of the boat and sank like a rock. As the water closed over the rabbi's head, one clergyman said to the other, "Do you think we should show him where the stepping-stones are?"

If you are trusting Jesus, you don't need to know where the stepping-stones are: You know the Stone. You step out on Him and you'll find He is the path to joy—joy that endures.

Praise be to the Lord, for he has heard my cry for mercy. The LORD is my strength and my shield; my heart trusts in him, and I am helped. My heart leaps for joy and I will give thanks to him in song. The Lord is the strength of his people. PSALM 28:6–8 NIV

But let all who take refuge in you be glad; let them ever sing for joy. Spread your protection over them, that those who love your name may rejoice in you. PSALM 5:11 NIV

Be filled with the Spirit;
Speaking to yourselves in
psalms and hymns and spiritual songs,
singing and making melody
in your heart to the Lord.

EPHESIANS 5:18–19

We will find delight if we live as a child of God. The Father's mind is ever thinking of us. His eyes are ever on us. He speaks words of healing comfort. His arms are strong enough to deliver us from any enemy while gentle enough to soothe any hurt. His heart is always faithful.

The Repentant Return

For years they had been slaves in a faraway country, their land despoiled, their temple pillaged and profaned. Worn by privations, heartsick, and homesick, they were gradually sifting home to the familiar hills for which they had long yearned.

Even as the fresh air of freedom wafted in their nostrils, the moldering ruin of their homeland brought tears to their eyes. Houses were heaps of rubble; fields were impenetrable thickets of thistle; their temple was utterly ravished. On every ruined hillock, on each impoverished plain, they saw the stark destruction that had befallen them and their land. The message from God to them was written on every pile of rocks: Judgment had fallen because of their sin. Now they wondered: Could God forgive them? Could their land be restored? Was there any hope?

Ezra, prophet, scribe, and priest, stood before the people. Their little makeshift temple courtyard was too small to hold the throng of searchers that had voluntarily gathered, so they met before the Water Gate, thirsting to hear the Book of the Law of God read aloud.

From morning to noon, Ezra read and expounded upon the ancient, familiar texts that described God's deliverance, righteousness, and promises. These were sacred words, hauntingly beautiful, yet they deeply wounded their already sin-weary souls. Could they escape further judgment when they had lived lives that were an offense to a righteous God? Was there no forgiveness? Tears of repentance turned to the weeping of desperation.

Then Nehemiah, their governor, stepped forward. "Do not grieve," he told them, "for the joy of the Lord is your strength" (Nehemiah 8:10).

Nehemiah's words are for you, too. You are aware of sins from the past. Perhaps you are living in difficult circumstances today because of those sins. Your life may be as devastated as the land of Israel was for the returning slaves.

But do not despair. Nehemiah's words are for every person who has sinned and had to live with the consequences of it: "The joy of the Lord is your strength."

What is the Lord's joy? Loving and forgiving you when you turn from your sins is what gives God joy. He delights in being the Great Salvager of ruined lives, including yours. He is pleased beyond measure to deliver you from sin's clutches and "restore the years that the locust have eaten" (Joel 2:25).

We give God joy when we turn our hearts back to Him. We give God joy when we worship and love Him. This is the joy that gave sweet fruit in that empty garden tomb.

For truly it is the most joy
that may be that He that is
highest and mightiest,
noblest and worthiest,
is lowest and meekest,
homeliest and most courteous:
and truly this marvelous joy
shall be shown us all
when we see Him.

JULIAN OF NORWICH

The First Taste of Satisfying Fruit

Alberto did not know it, but he was a marked man. The God Squad had him in their sights.

"The God Squad" was comprised of five blue-collar workers who labored in a large, midwestern manufacturing plant. The two founding members, Nick and George, had long regarded the factory where they worked as their mission field. To arm for battle with Satan, they named themselves "The God Squad" and met for a half hour prior to their shift to pray that the other men on their line would find the Lord. Over the years, they had the privilege of leading several men to the Lord, and three of those began joining them for their early prayer time.

The reason they targeted Alberto was simple: "He was mean, angry, and swore fluently in two languages," said Nick. "I couldn't stand to hear him use the Lord's name like that! He was either going to get saved or I was afraid I was going to punch him in the mouth! So we prayed, 'Lord, smite him with Your love!' "

The five men prayed for Alberto and looked for chances to witness. Their opportunity came when Alberto was arrested for beating up his wife. She received a restraining order against him. Meanwhile, a long way from his native Texas, Alberto was totally disconnected from his family for the first time.

"I loved my wife and kids," said Alberto. "You probably couldn't have told it by the way I treated them, but I did love them. I wanted to get them back, and I knew Nick, George, and the others were religious, so I started eating lunch with them, hoping they'd tell God to make my wife let me come home. I know that wasn't right, but that was my plan."

Alberto, instead, got five new friends who invited him to their church and their homes. "They boldly testified to me about the life-changing power of Jesus and the joy of the Holy Spirit, both on and off the job," said Alberto. "They told me I was a sinner and that I needed Jesus. I was so lonely and unhappy I would have signed up for Amway or anything that promised to give me happiness. But after I prayed the sinner's prayer, I found forgiveness and a deep-down happiness and satisfaction I'd never known. My problems—or my temper—didn't go away; I could just handle them better with the Lord's help."

Alberto's wife was suspicious of his newly found faith. She had been through one too many of Alberto's cycles of abuse and regret; she was planning on moving back to Texas and leaving him behind.

"When I knew she was leaving," said Alberto, "I literally begged God for help. He impressed on me to do something I had never done before: ask for forgiveness. I couldn't go over to the house, so I called my family on the telephone—and then I asked my wife and kids to forgive me, no strings attached. God told me I wasn't supposed to beg them to stay in the North or to take me back. All I needed to do was ask them to forgive me."

Strange things began to occur. One delay after another kept Alberto's wife and children from leaving the area. During that time, Alberto spent as much time with his family as his wife would allow.

"She would need me for something. The first time she called was when the toilet overflowed. You wouldn't think an overflowed toilet would be an answer to prayer, but it was!" Alberto laughed. "She was nervous about having me at the house, and when it turned out that one of the little kids had flushed a potato down the john and plugged it, she thought I'd lose my temper for sure! But I didn't. Then after that, she'd call for one reason or another. Slowly, she could see I'd changed."

Alberto's family is now restored, attending church together, and he has joined the other members of the God Squad in claiming their factory workplace for the Lord.

"I can't believe how many years I've wasted being unhappy," said Alberto. "Now that I have died to my own life, I have finally experienced the joy of Christ's resurrection. I'm grateful I now have eternity to live in God's joy!"

Study always to have Joy, for it befits not the servant of God to show before his brother or another sadness or a troubled face. FRANCIS OF ASSISI

The Joyous Fruit of the Lord

Helen is a woman who loves the Lord. Despite a difficult marriage to an irascible tyrant, she maintains a sweet spirit as she cares for him and extends hospitality to his extended family. His constant demands take a toll on her health and peace of mind, but she carefully tries to keep her heart right with God and frequently requests prayer for her attitude toward her husband.

Because of this, I was surprised to hear her comment that sometimes she was afraid to pray. "Sometimes when I go to pray, all I can think of is all of the bad things I've done and thought. I feel so guilty," she said, "that I can hardly pray. Even when I've repented of those sins, I can't stand to be in His presence.

"Then one day I realized what was happening: Satan, the accuser, was constantly reminding me of my forgiven sins and lying to me that God had not forgiven me! He was doing that to keep me from praying and to make me avoid God's presence.

"But I know Jesus died for my sins and rose again so that I can be forgiven! Now, when I get those feelings, I tell Satan, 'You're a liar! God has forgiven me! That sin is covered by the blood of Jesus, and I can joyfully stand in the presence of God.' "

There is therefore now no condemnation to them which are in Christ Jesus. . . . For the law of the Spirit of life in Christ Jesus hath made me free. . . . ROMANS 8:1–2

The Enduring Fruit of Joy

The picture is a typical example of early 1950s color photography. Although the paper is browned slightly by the patina of time, the hues are still a little garish and exaggerated. In the photo, a skinny girl in pajamas sits next to a Christmas tree hugging a doll baby. Her enthralled expression is that of newly budded maternal love mixed with joy.

"Oh, I remember the moment very well," Grace said, tapping the photo with her polished nail. Over the years, the skinny girl had metamorphosed into this elegant matron who was looking forward to soon becoming a grandmother.

"I wanted that doll so badly, and it had to be that particular doll. But my parents were poor, and there were a lot of kids in my family. I told my parents what I wanted, but I also prayed God to give it to me. You see, I knew that God was better situated financially than my parents, so I focused my nagging on God," she laughed.

Grace prayed every night for that particular doll, and when requests were made at her church's prayer meeting, she raised her hand and asked that everyone pray she get that doll for Christmas.

"The congregation tittered," said Grace, "but I really didn't care. It was the desire of my heart. I felt like I just had to have that doll. You see, it seemed like a real baby to me. My baby."

From the moment she saw that doll baby until Christmas, time dragged slowly for Grace. "I just couldn't wait until Christmas! It seemed like December twenty-fifth would never come," she said. But when it did, Grace was almost afraid to open her few presents.

"I thought, *What if I don't get that doll? How am I going to act happy so my parents won't be sad?* You see, I knew if I didn't get the doll, it would be because my parents just couldn't afford it, and I didn't want to ruin their Christmas."

But on Christmas morning when she opened the box and found the doll, her father had his camera ready for the moment. "It required real sacrifice on their part to get the doll, but I loved that doll baby. I didn't care if I didn't get another doll. I played and played with it. I still have it."

The doll and picture again became important to Grace after she grew into an adult. "When my husband and I couldn't have children, I put this photo in my Bible," she said. "When I prayed for a child, I would get out this picture and remind myself how God had answered my prayer then. I thought, *If I'm going to ask God for a baby, I had better act on faith that He's going to send me one!* So I bought a bassinet and put the doll in it. And I bought a rocking chair, too. Whenever I would get lonely for my baby that had not yet arrived, I would rock the doll and thank God for His promises. My husband thought I was cracking up!"

In due season, Grace's faith was rewarded, not once, but four times! She showed me a photo of herself holding her firstborn. Again, her face registered the same emotions as the one taken so long ago—the joy that comes in the morning.

All of us go through dark nights when our dearest hopes are put to death. But Resurrection joy comes in the morning.

> *There is, above all, . . .the joy of making the world new. . . laughter from triumph over pain and hardship. . .the joy of bringing the light of truth and beauty into a dark world.* JOHN BOODIN

> *For then shalt thou have thy delight in the Almighty, and shalt lift up thy face unto God.* JOB 22:26

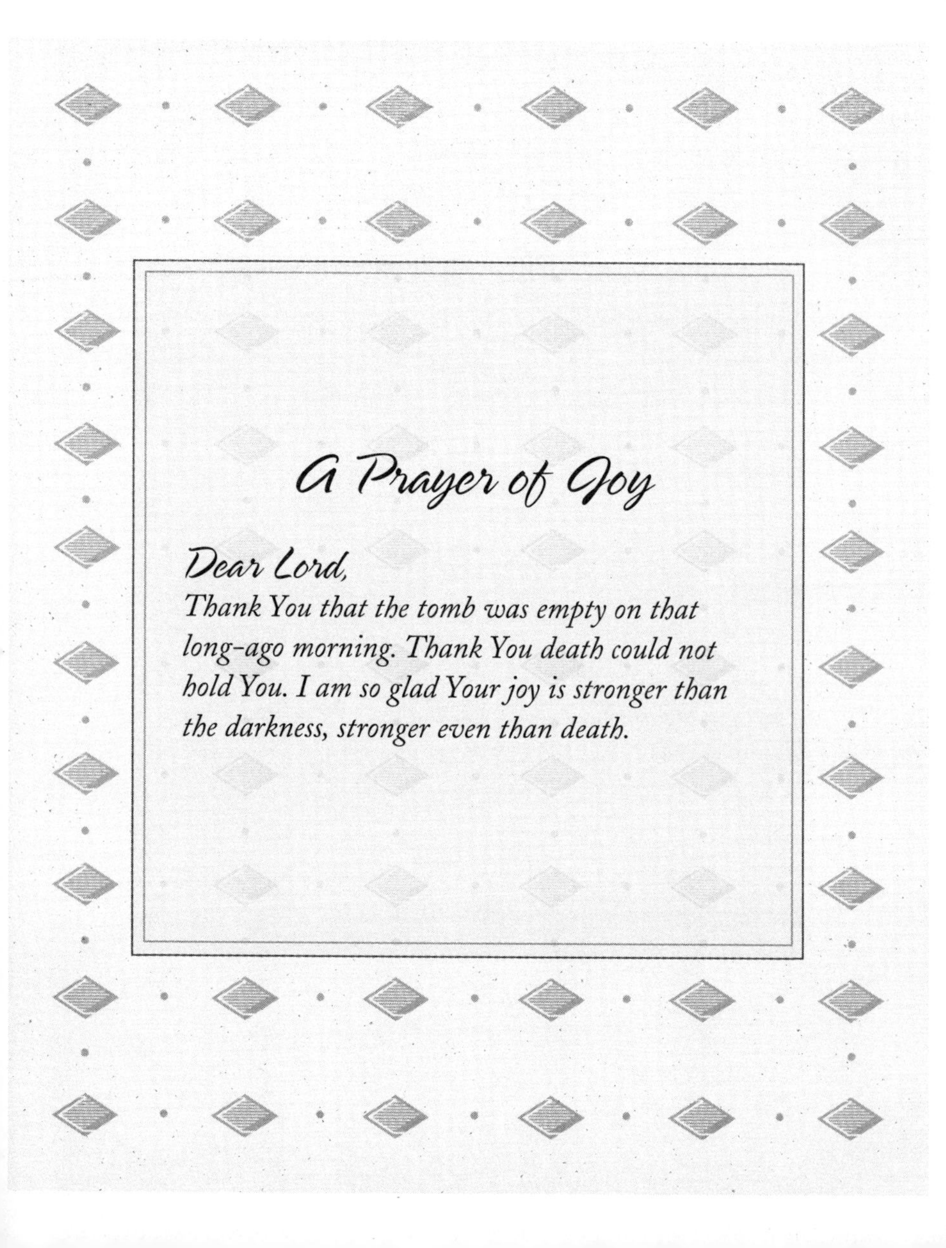

A Prayer of Joy

Dear Lord,

Thank You that the tomb was empty on that long-ago morning. Thank You death could not hold You. I am so glad Your joy is stronger than the darkness, stronger even than death.

Chapter 7

Eternal Growth: A Joy That Grows Forever

Give light to my eyes, or I will sleep in death; my enemy will say, "I have overcome him," and my foes will rejoice when I fall. But I trust in your unfailing love; my heart rejoices in your salvation. I will sing to the LORD, for he has been good to me. PSALM 13:3-6 NIV

Do not rejoice that the spirits submit to you, but rejoice that your names are written in heaven.

LUKE 10:20 NIV

Earthly joys will always be marred by regret. Heavenly joys will be complete with nothing to scar them. In this life we can only glimpse the wonderful, amazing harvest of joy that will be ours for all eternity.

Eternal Joy

Rejoice in the Lord alway:
and again I say, Rejoice.

PHILIPPIANS 4:4

Paul wrote these words from a damp, Roman jail cell where he awaited an audience with Nero, Emperor of Rome and certifiable fiend. Paul knew well Nero's proclivity for torturing Christians. He had no doubt Nero would see him as a leader of these hated people and thus worthy of a sadistically cruel death. Facing this, Paul wrote his final advice to the persecuted church in Philippi: "Rejoice in the Lord always; and again I say, Rejoice!"

Paul knew that the life of a follower of Christ would be torn by danger, yet he said, "Rejoice in the Lord always!" He knew that the believer might face rejection from those whom he loved, but Paul still encouraged, "Rejoice in the Lord always!"

Paul knew this joy, experienced this joy, and lived day in, day out immersed in this joy, because he lived in the presence of Christ. He could face anything as long as his Beloved was by his side. He knew that for him death would mean merely the entrance into joy that was still greater and deeper, more brilliant than anything this life could ever offer.

We are made for eternity. . . .

A.W. TOZER

This short, earthly life, important and significant though it may be in its setting, is no more than a prelude to a share in the timeless Life of God. J. B. PHILLIPS

Enduring Joy

If our eyes were opened into the spirit world, if the veil that separates the physical from the eternal were jerked back so we could see beyond, we would see an amazing universe that exists around us.

We would see the angels of God defending our souls from the hosts of Satan. We would see the "hosts of witnesses," those who have died in faith before us and now encourage us to run with confidence toward an eternity of joy with Jesus. We might see the treasures we have laid up in heaven by what we have done for God.

But shining brighter than heavenly treasure, more glorious than the redeemed, with power and majesty far beyond the angels, we would see Jesus. We would see that everywhere we go He stays beside us. When we need wisdom, we only have to ask Him because He is there. When we need direction, if we look to Him, His nail-scarred hands point out the next step. When we are lonely, He is ever present. Discouraged? He lifts us up. Sad? He comforts. Defeated? He gives victory. Needy? He supplies. Sick? He heals. Whatever our need, He supplies.

He is the source of all joy. And the joy He gives is permanent, solid, enduring. No wonder the Scriptures say if we don't rejoice in Him the rocks will cry out!

How good is man's life,
the mere living!
how fit to employ
All the heart and the soul and the
senses forever in joy!
ROBERT BROWNING

God longs to give us joy. Joy is a part of His very nature. It is woven into Creation—and it will spring up in our hearts for eternity when we open ourselves to the Holy Spirit.

Live near to God,
and all things will appear
little to you in comparison with
eternal realities.

ROBERT MURRAY MCCHEYNE

The eternal life is not the future life; it is life in harmony with the true order of things—life in God.

HENRI AMIEL

In love we start eternity right here below.

Henri de Lubac

The greatest blessedness is to know God in the clear light of eternal life—seeing Him truly, experiencing Him tenderly, possessing Him completely in the fullness of joy.

. . .I hope that by His Grace He will continue to draw our outward appearance more and more into conformity with our inward gladness, making us all one with Him and with each other in the true and eternal joy which is Jesus.

Julian of Norwich

A Prayer for Eternal Joy

Our Father which art in heaven (Matthew 6:9), *who is like You who dwells on high?* (Psalm 113:5).

I will not fear, because I am one of Your flock. It is Your good pleasure as my Father to give me a place in Your Kingdom (Luke 12:32).

Jesus is preparing a place for me in Your house where there are many mansions. He will come again and receive me to Himself, that where He is, I will be also (John 14:2–3).

When I stand in Your presence, You will wipe away all tears from my eyes; and there shall be no

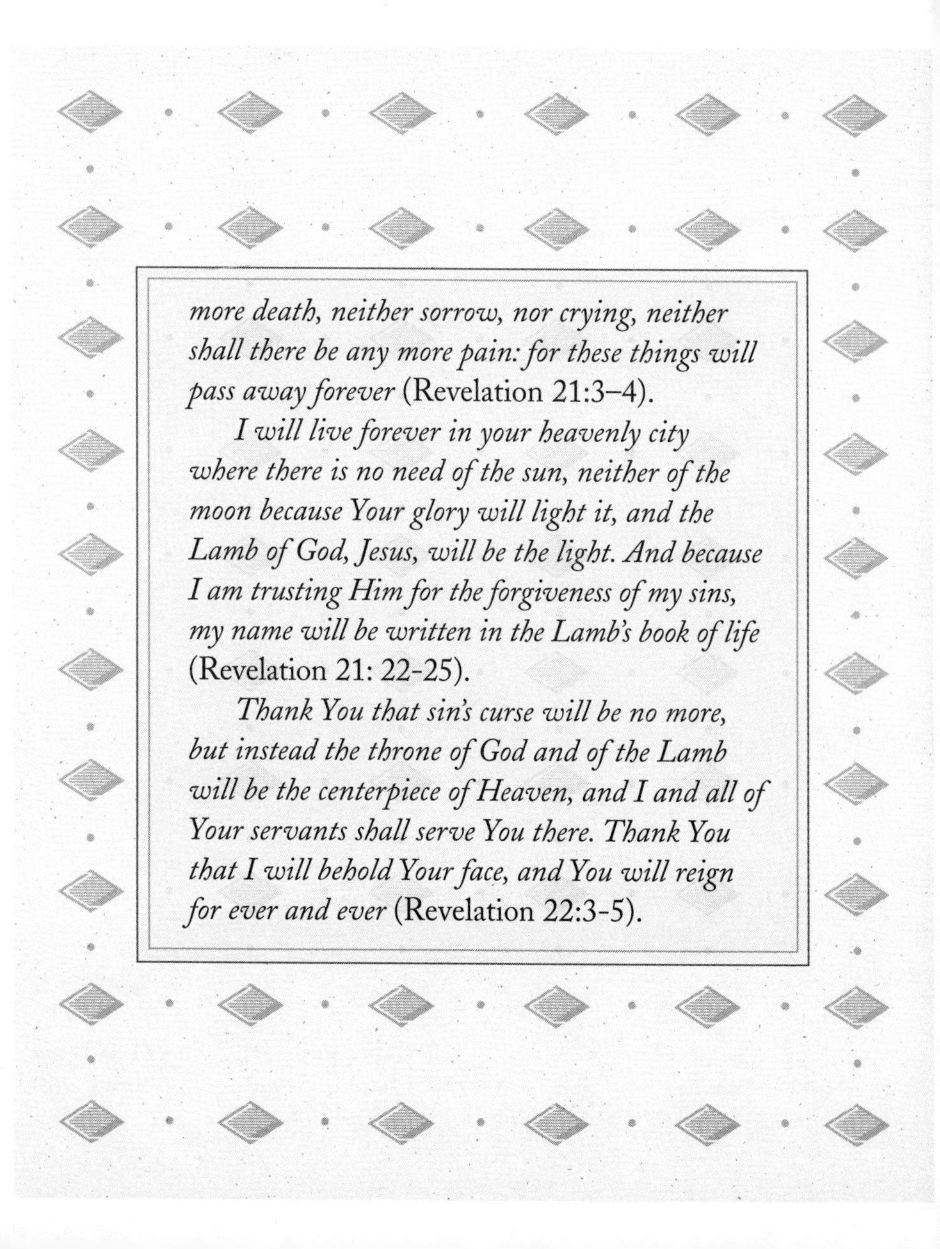

more death, neither sorrow, nor crying, neither shall there be any more pain: for these things will pass away forever (Revelation 21:3–4).

I will live forever in your heavenly city where there is no need of the sun, neither of the moon because Your glory will light it, and the Lamb of God, Jesus, will be the light. And because I am trusting Him for the forgiveness of my sins, my name will be written in the Lamb's book of life (Revelation 21: 22-25).

Thank You that sin's curse will be no more, but instead the throne of God and of the Lamb will be the centerpiece of Heaven, and I and all of Your servants shall serve You there. Thank You that I will behold Your face, and You will reign for ever and ever (Revelation 22:3-5).

For ye shall go out with joy,
and be led forth with peace:
the mountains and the hills
shall break forth
before you into singing,
and all the trees of the field
shall clap their hands.

ISAIAH 55:12

About the Author

Rebekah Montgomery has over thirty years of experience as a pastor and teacher. A prolific writer, she is the author of several books; many magazine, newspaper, and inspirational articles; camp and Bible school curriculum; and children's musicals. Rebekah is the author of *Ordinary Miracles: True Stories of an Extraordinary God Who Works in Our Everyday Lives* (Promise Press, May 2000), and is presently developing a book series on the *Fruit of the Spirit* (Promise Press, July 2000).

Rebekah lives in Kewanee, Illinois, with John, her husband of thirty years, and their three children, Mary, Joel, and Daniel.